Praise for *Positive Discipline in th*

"Placing the accent on helpful solutions rather than just consequences has made it possible for us to raise our vision to a new level of mutual respect and cooperation in our class meetings. As an added and much-appreciated benefit, we have found that applying the principles of class meetings—compliments and thank-yous, an open agenda in which all may participate, and looking for solutions rather than blame—to our faculty meetings has dramatically improved them as well, leading to a closer, more supportive faculty."

Mike Brock, principal
Mary Immaculate School
Farmers Branch, Texas

"As producers of *The Video Journal of Education,* we had searched for a powerful discipline program, one that would place the responsibility for behavior with children and give students life skills for dealing with problems. After looking at many programs, we were very excited to discover *Positive Discipline in the Classroom.* It met our criteria perfectly. We have visited many schools that have implemented Positive Discipline, and it has been our observation that teachers and administrators love it because it works, and students love the empowering influence that *Positive Discipline in the Classroom* brings to them."

Blanch Linton, president
The Video Journal of Education

"*Positive Discipline in the Classroom* is a treasure for all members of the learning community. As we reexamine our schools, the principles put forth in this book need to be at the center of our thinking. Class meetings must be a part of all classrooms, . . . and the concepts of mistaken goals and use of barriers and builders must be household words for all members of the learning community. I applaud the authors for presenting these ideas and many more in such a user-friendly format."

Kathryn Fithian Markovchick, Ph.D., director
Maine Support Network
Readfield, Maine

"When our school was first introduced to the *Positive Discipline in the Classroom* program in 1994, we adopted it immediately. Our schoolwide discipline program affects all students, encouraging them to solve problems, resolve conflicts, and take responsibility for their own actions. We were excited to hear about the revised edition of *Positive Discipline in the Classroom,* which encourages children (and adults) even further to communicate with each other about their problems and work toward finding solutions."

Kris Richards, M.S., school counselor
Lakewood Elementary School
Lakewood, Washington

". . . thank you for writing *Positive Discipline in the Classroom.* Each day we both encounter many situations in which conflict-resolution skills are necessary. Having learned our own skills through trial and error, we realize the importance of teaching children a constructive way of dealing with conflict. We feel strongly that problem-solving skills are necessary in every aspect of our lives. . . . We are encouraging schools to adopt problem-solving systems such as those described in *Positive Discipline in the Classroom.*"

Lyndon Taylor, attorney, and
Pamela Taylor, former college professor
Houston, Texas

▼

Positive Discipline in the Classroom

Revised and Expanded Second Edition

Jane Nelsen, Ed.D., M.F.C.C.
Lynn Lott, M.A., M.F.C.C.
H. Stephen Glenn

Prima Publishing

PRIMA PUBLISHING and colophon are registered trademarks of Prima Communications, Inc.

Lyrics from the song "Number One" are reprinted with permission from Songs for Elementary Emotional Development by Wayne Frieden and Marie Hartwell-Walker. Copyright 1992 by Education Research Associates, P.O. Box 7678-J, Amherst, MA 01004.

Library of Congress Cataloging-in-Publication Data

Nelsen, Jane.
    Positive discipline in the classroom / Jane Nelsen, Lynn Lott, and H. Stephen Glenn. —Rev. and expanded 2nd ed.
        p.   cm.
    Includes bibliographical references and index.
    ISBN 0-7615-1059-1
    1. Classroom management—United States.   2. School discipline—United States.   I. Lott, Lynn.   II. Glenn, H. Stephen.
III. Title.
LB3013.N4   1997
371.5'3—dc21   97-9016
                                                                          CIP

97 98 99 00 01 HH 10 9 8 7 6 5 4 3 2 1
Printed in the United States of America

How to Order
Single copies may be ordered from Prima Publishing, P.O. Box 1260BK, Rocklin, CA 95677; telephone (916) 632-4400. Quantity discounts are also available. On your letterhead, include information concerning the intended use of the books and the number of books you wish to purchase.

Visit us online at http://www.primapublishing.com

To Alfred Adler and Rudolf Dreikurs for their theories of mutual respect, and to the hundreds of school personnel and students who have confirmed the value of these theories in schools.

A special thanks to those people who have taken our ideas and used them in more creative ways than we ever imagined.

▼

Contents

Introduction   *ix*

Chapter 1   The Positive Discipline Dream   1

Chapter 2   The Message of Caring   17

Chapter 3   Building Blocks for Effective
             Class Meetings   37

Chapter 4   Strengthening Communication Skills   57

Chapter 5   Why People Do What They Do   71

Chapter 6   Effective Problem-Solving Skills   87

Chapter 7   Focusing on Solutions Instead
             of Punishment   101

Chapter 8   Putting It All Together   113

Chapter 9   Expanding Class-Meeting Skills   121

Chapter 10   Questions and Answers About
             Class Meetings   135

Chapter 11   Positive Discipline Classroom
             Management Tools   159

Chapter 12   Teachers Helping Teachers
             Problem-Solving Steps and
             Encouragement Meetings   185

Appendix: *When Logical Consequences*
             Are Appropriate   *203*

             Bibliography   *211*

             Index   *215*

▼

Introduction

We often hear the cry, "Back to basics!" We agree. However, we disagree with many on their definition of "the basics." We do not believe the basics are reading, writing, and arithmetic. We believe the basics are courage, confidence, and life skills.[1] When children have these basics, they have fertile ground on which to learn academics and to live successfully in the world.

In the United States, the federal law requiring children to attend school says nothing about reading, writing, and arithmetic; it says that the purpose of education is "to prepare children for responsible citizenship." Reading, writing, and arithmetic do not prepare young people for responsible citizenship. All the academic knowledge in the world will not help those who lack self-discipline, judgment, social interest, the ability to make good choices, and the sense of responsibility that enables them to act effectively in life. Unfortunately, our educational

---

1. Daniel Goleman, author of *Emotional Intelligence* (New York: Bantam, 1995), reports that research has discovered emotional intelligence (EQ) to be vastly important to success in life; it is defined as skills in empathy, cooperation, persuasion, and consensus building as well as the ability to read one's feelings, to control one's impulses and anger, to calm oneself down, and to maintain resolve and hope in the face of setbacks.

According to an article published September 11, 1995, in the *Corpus Christi Caller Times*, the research goes on to state that, "Emotional intelligence appears to be in startling decline among American children. This across-the-board drop in children's emotional intelligence is in many ways a more

system today simply does not provide young people with these skills.

Positive Discipline in the Classroom is a program that prepares children for responsible citizenship. It is a program that encourages the development of emotional intelligence and the important life skills and perceptions of capable people (the Significant Seven) as outlined in chapter 1.

In this book we emphasize the importance of class meetings. Although the program includes additional methods, teachers have discovered that class meetings teach essential skills and empower young people with a positive attitude for success in all areas of life: school, work, family, and society. Students learn social skills, such as listening, taking turns, hearing different points of view, negotiating, communicating, helping one another, and taking responsibility for their own behavior. They also strengthen their academic skills, perhaps without realizing it. During class meetings students learn oral language skills, attentiveness, critical-thinking skills, decision-making skills, problem-solving skills, and democratic procedures, all of which will enhance their academic performance. Many teachers find that the class-meeting process exceeds curriculum goals for social studies, language development, and health and safety, because student involvement in problem solving means that students

---

troubling trend than a dip in the SAT taken for college admission. Deficits in EQ are linked with a range of social perils (such as dropping out of school, fighting, delinquency, drug use, teen pregnancy, and eating disorders). The rate of decline (in EQ) was the same for all, privileged and impoverished children alike."

Goleman goes on to report that, "Children in courses (addressing EQ skills) show marked improvements in the ability to control their impulses, show empathy, cooperate with others, manage anger and anxiety, focus on a task, pursue goals, and resolve conflicts. Delinquency, fights, and drug use drop. And there is an added bonus: achievement test scores rise too."

are no longer passive recipients of the teacher's knowledge. Active participation in the learning process leads to deeper understanding and promotes inner motivation and commitment to appropriate action.

Reading, writing, and arithmetic are more meaningful in students' lives after they acquire the skills they can learn through class meetings. The experience of class meetings helps students become more receptive to learning what the educational system has to offer.

For years we've watched as schools look for methods to handle classroom discipline. When the underlying motivation of discipline is control and punishment rather than an opportunity for learning, little will be accomplished. What has happened in many of our schools is sad and frightening. In a workshop at the North American Society of Adlerian Psychologists in June 1992, Dr. William Nicoll discussed the "pathological environment" created in many of our schools. With some irony he identified "new categories" of mental illness that are created in the school environment.

Dr. Nicoll calls his first category Classroom-Induced School Phobia. This condition expresses itself by persistent, excessive worry about school and a fear of doing something or acting in a way that could be humiliating or embarrassing, possibly resulting in disapproval or rejection. The problem may be accompanied by headaches, stomachaches, decreased social functioning outside school, verbalized fears of poor performance, fear of the teacher, nightmares, sleep disturbances, depression, and a refusal to attend school.

After describing several more school-induced anxiety and mood disorders, Dr. Nicoll sums up with a description of what he calls Adult Children of Dysfunctional Classrooms, or ACDCs. These adults become agitated when faced with new tasks, responsibilities, or challenges; they suffer flashbacks involving past classroom traumas, such as failure, perceived humiliation, and loss of prestige. Adult Children of Dysfunctional Classrooms may also avoid risk taking, experience feelings of inferiority or inadequacy, or possess generalized anger and resentment toward educators.

It is possible to turn this negativity around, but it takes both time and commitment to change the atmosphere in our schools and classrooms as well as our basic beliefs about the educational system. We need to move away from a system based on competition, in which success is for the few and being a success is at someone else's expense. We must move toward developing competency and self-worth, accompanied by responsible decision making and helping one another. In this atmosphere, schools can empower young people with courage, confidence, and life skills instead of burdening them with feelings of fear and inadequacy.

We, the authors, are educators committed to providing the tools that can help teachers, administrators, and parents bring health to an unhealthy system. Together we have over seventy-five years of experience in lecturing, writing, counseling, and teaching others to create families and classrooms where both adults and children feel encouraged and empowered to accept themselves and others and to work together for the good of all. In this book we have combined our resources to share our ideas about how to change the school environment into an atmosphere of learning and respect.

▼

Chapter

I

The Positive Discipline Dream

The proper way of training children is identical with the
proper way of treating fellow human beings.

Rudolf Dreikurs

We have a dream. The dream is about schools where
young people are treated with respect and have the opportunity to learn the skills they need for a successful life. The
dream is about schools where children will never experience humiliation when they fail but will instead feel
empowered by the opportunity to learn from their mistakes in a safe environment. It is a dream about schools
where students learn cooperation instead of competition,
where students and teachers collaborate on solutions.
The dream is about students and teachers helping one
another to create an environment that inspires excite-
ment for life and learning because fear and feelings of

1

inadequacy and discouragement are no longer part of the learning environment. The end result is an educational system that nurtures young people and gives them the skills and attitudes that will help them be happy, contributing members of society.

Many teachers and students have realized this dream by using methods based on mutual respect. Mutual respect requires that adults see children as people and as unique individuals. Teachers who see students this way do not treat them as robots whose only function is to be controlled and manipulated "for their own good." They see students as valuable resources with worthwhile ideas and skills.

Mutual respect is a two-way street. It invites young people to see adults as people who need nurturing and encouragement just as much as students do. They will see this only when it is modeled for them. A climate for mutual respect is created when teachers allow students to become involved in ways in which they can listen to one another, take each other seriously, and work together to solve problems for the benefit of all. In a climate of mutual respect, students are treated as assets with much to contribute. Teachers don't have to "do it all" when they teach the skills of cooperation and contribution and allow students to help. Teachers don't have to "act controlling" when all are working together respectfully.

Creating a Positive Discipline classroom is a process of putting together parts of a puzzle. The parts include creating an atmosphere of caring based on kindness and firmness, dignity and mutual respect; using Positive Discipline classroom management tools; understanding the Four Mistaken Goals of Behavior; collaborating with other faculty to adopt the Teachers Helping Teachers Problem-Solving Steps and Encouragement Meetings; holding parent/teacher/student conferences to communicate progress and find ways to encourage students; holding regularly scheduled classroom meetings; and using encouragement through supportive feedback. Each of these methods will be discussed thoroughly in later chapters.

Our primary focus in this book is to show how students and teachers together can create a classroom climate that is nurturing to both self-esteem and academic performance. Since the class meeting provides the greatest potential for teaching children empowering life skills in the least amount of time, we will devote several chapters to teaching the eight building blocks for effective class meetings. Every one of these chapters includes methods and skills that can be used by teachers and students throughout the day as well as in class meetings.[1]

Because we understand the incredible benefits of class meetings for teachers and students who use them, we are amazed by the resistance to them from school personnel who have not yet discovered their positive effects. Following are some comments we have heard from teachers and administrators as they briefed us before in-service training.

> Teachers don't want you to spend much time on class meetings. They would prefer you talk about involving kids in their education, getting kids to think for themselves, and helping teachers deal with students who act out.
>
> Students don't like to sit around in a circle discussing problems. It's not their way.

---

1. For hundreds of other Positive Discipline methods, please refer to Jane Nelsen, Roslyn Duffy, Linda Escobar, Kate Ortolano, and Debbie Owen-Sohocki, *Positive Discipline in the Classroom: A Teacher's A–Z Guide* (Rocklin, Calif.: Prima, 1996); Jane Nelsen and Lynn Lott, *Positive Discipline for Teenagers* (Rocklin, Calif.: Prima, 1994); Lynn Lott and Riki Intner, *The Family That Works Together . . .* (Rocklin, Calif.: Prima, 1994); and Jane Nelsen, *Positive Discipline*, rev. ed. (New York: Ballantine, 1996).

> Don't waste our time on class meetings. Some of us teach high school classes that are fifty minutes long, and we don't have time to waste on meetings.
>
> Junior high students are incapable of holding class meetings without insulting each other and being silly.

These teachers and administrators do not know that all of their concerns can be addressed and solved through the class-meeting process. A well-run class meeting involves students in their education, teaches them to think for themselves, and eliminates most problems with students who act out.[2]

Those who experience belonging and significance through participation in class meetings seldom need to misbehave. (For more about misbehavior see chapter 5.) When they do misbehave, students can learn to help each other, usually with more effective results than when they are referred to sources outside the classroom.

Too often, if students are having difficulty in the classroom, it is assumed that the causes are learning disabilities or behavioral problems that exist solely within the students. At other times, it is assumed that the causes lie with their families. It has become popular to "solve" these problems by sending students to the principal, a counselor, or a school psychologist for referral to a special education program.

When classroom teachers learn to implement effective class meetings, most problems can be handled successfully through the class-meeting process instead of being referred to other sources. Students are taught a fundamental concept: "There are enough of us here to help each other; we don't need to pass the buck." Some teach-

---

2. *Positive Discipline in the Classroom* by Video Journal shows several examples of well-run class meetings in which students (in kindergarten through high school classrooms from all over the country) treat each other with dignity and respect and help each other find nonpunitive solutions to problems. For information, call 1-800-456-7770.

ers are surprised when students decide for themselves on a solution the teacher has tried to implement unsuccessfully or with continual reminders. With training, students seem more willing to listen to each other than to adults. The truth is that when they are respectfully involved, they take ownership of and responsibility for the solutions they help create. Class meetings provide a supportive atmosphere for students to become actively involved in determining their needs and implementing strategies they design to benefit everyone concerned. Students can come up with wonderfully creative solutions when given the opportunity.

Another alternative to referring students to outside sources is the piece of the Positive Discipline in the Classroom puzzle called Teachers Helping Teachers Problem-Solving Steps (covered in chapter 12), in which teachers learn to encourage each other and act as consultants to each other as they brainstorm ideas to encourage discouraged students. In this process, teachers help each other find practical ways to use all of the Positive Discipline methods taught throughout this book.

What Do You Really Want for Your Students?

In our two-day training workshops for Positive Discipline in the Classroom,[3] we ask teachers, "What characteristics and skills do you think children need in order to be happy, contributing (successful) members of society?" The observers are always similar: responsibility, respect for self and others, self-discipline, self-control, concern for others, self-esteem, self-confidence, risk taking,

---

3. For more information on these workshops, please call Jane Nelsen at (916) 338-5551 or Lynn Lott at (707) 526-3141, Ext. 3#.

capability, confidence, happiness, communication skills, problem-solving skills, sense of humor, motivation to learn, compassion, etc. We then ask, "Are these characteristics and skills as important as math, reading, or science?" The answer is a unanimous, "More important." The next question is obvious: "How can teachers say they don't have time to spend helping children develop these important characteristics and skills?"

When teachers use the class-meeting process and other parts of the Positive Discipline puzzle, students have the opportunity to develop every one of these characteristics and skills. And when they have these characteristics and skills, discipline problems are eliminated and students have more enthusiasm for the academic process.

The Significant Seven

Many teachers have told us that discipline problems are significantly reduced when they use class meetings and other Positive Discipline methods. Some teachers may want to implement Positive Discipline methods for this reason alone. However, we firmly believe that eliminating discipline problems is only the fringe benefit of following these methods. The major benefits are the social, academic, and life skills students experience, which can be summed up in what we call the Significant Seven[4]. Notice that the Significant Seven are similar to the characteristics and skills brainstormed by teachers when asked what they want for their students. The Significant Seven are the following three empowering perceptions and four essential skills.

---

4. A chapter on each component of the Significant Seven can be found in H. Stephen Glenn and Jane Nelsen, *Raising Self-Reliant Children in a Self-Indulgent World* (Rocklin, Calif.: Prima, 1989) and are taught in the Developing Capable People Course. Call (916) 338-6662 for more information.

Three Empowering Perceptions

1. Perceptions of personal capabilities: "I am capable."
2. Perceptions of significance in primary relationships: "I contribute in meaningful ways, and I am genuinely needed."
3. Perceptions of personal power of influence over life: "I can influence what happens to me."

Four Essential Skills

1. Intrapersonal skills: the ability to understand personal emotions, to use that understanding to develop self-discipline and self-control, and to learn from experiences.
2. Interpersonal skills: the ability to work with others through listening, communicating, cooperating, negotiating, sharing, and empathizing.
3. Systemic skills: the ability to respond to the limits and consequences of everyday life with responsibility, adaptability, flexibility, and integrity.
4. Judgment skills: the ability to develop wisdom and evaluate situations according to appropriate values.

Students who are weak in the development of these seven significant perceptions and skills are at high risk for the serious problems facing youth, such as drug abuse, teen pregnancy, suicide, delinquency, and gang involvement. Students with strength in the Significant Seven are at low risk for serious problems. Obviously, it is extremely important that young people have the opportunity to develop the Significant Seven, and the class meeting provides an excellent opportunity in the following ways:

1. To develop a perception of personal capability, young people need a safe climate where they can experiment with learning and behavior without judgments

about success or failure. Positive Discipline methods provide a safe climate where students can examine their behavior, discover how it affects others, and engage in effective problem solving.

2. To develop a perception of significance in primary relationships, young people need the experience of having others listen to their feelings, thoughts, and ideas and take them seriously. In a Positive Discipline classroom, everyone has the opportunity to voice opinions and give suggestions. Students learn that they can contribute significantly to the problem-solving process and can successfully follow through on chosen suggestions.

3. To develop a perception of power and influence over their lives, young people need the opportunity to contribute in useful ways. They can learn to understand and accept the power they have to create a positive (or a negative) environment. They also learn that even when they can't control what happens, they can control their response to what happens and their choice of resulting actions.

4. A Positive Discipline classroom provides an excellent opportunity for the development of intrapersonal skills. Young people seem to be more willing to listen to one another than to adults. They gain understanding of their personal emotions and behaviors by hearing feedback from their classmates. In a nonthreatening climate, young people are willing to be accountable for their actions. They learn to separate their feelings from their actions and the results of their actions. They can learn that what they feel (anger, for instance) is separate from what they do (hit someone), and that while feelings are always acceptable, some actions are not. Through the problem-solving process, they learn alternative ways to express or deal with their thoughts or feelings. They develop self-discipline and self-control by thinking through the conse-

quences of their choices and by accepting suggestions for solutions from other students.

5. A Positive Discipline classroom provides the best possible opportunity for young people to develop inter-personal skills through dialogue and sharing, listening and empathizing, cooperation, negotiation, and conflict resolution. Instead of stepping in and resolving problems for students, teachers can suggest putting the problem on the class-meeting agenda or using the Four Problem-Solving Steps (discussed in chapter 11), where students and teachers can work on a win-win solution together.

6. In a Positive Discipline classroom, young people develop excellent systemic skills by responding to the limits and consequences of everyday life with responsibility, adaptability, flexibility, and integrity because they do not experience punishment or disapproval. A Positive Discipline classroom provides a place where kids know it's okay to make mistakes and learn from them. They learn that it's safe to take responsibility for their mistakes because they will not experience blame, shame, or pain. They learn to give up the victim mentality of blaming others ("the teacher gave me an F") and accept an accountability mentality ("I received an F because I didn't do the work").

7. Young people develop judgment skills only when they have opportunities and encouragement to practice making choices and decisions in an environment that emphasizes learning from mistakes instead of "paying" for mistakes through some kind of punishment. In a Positive Discipline classroom, students explore what happened, what caused it to happen, how behavior affects others, and what they can do to prevent or solve problems.

Too many adults expect children to develop wisdom and sound judgment without the opportunity to practice, make mistakes, learn, and try again. Regular class meetings give young people a lot of practice time. When teachers understand the relevance of the Significant Seven, they know how important it is to provide students with opportunities to develop strength in these empowering perception and essential skill areas.

A foundation of mutual respect and student involvement is imperative. The old methods of punishment, humiliation, and control do not work. It is a rare teacher who does not see the value of teaching the skills and attitudes we have discussed in our dream to empower young people. Most teachers would prefer to give up punishment and external control if they had the skills to help students learn self-control, self-discipline, responsibility, and problem-solving skills. However, making the changes necessary to realize the dream may not be easy for teachers or for students.

Positive Change for Future Dividends

Many teachers are accustomed to directing students, and many students are used to being directed by teachers. It takes time to break ineffective habits and replace them with empowering habits. Expect some reluctance as you begin the process of helping students develop the capacity to solve their own problems.

One of the most difficult changes for some teachers is seeing the value of taking ten to thirty minutes out of their academic schedule to spend on class meetings. Conversely, teachers who have experienced the short- and long-range benefits of these meetings wonder how they survived without them. It is interesting to note that even though teachers acknowledge that the characteristics and skills children need for success in life are even more important than academics, they are often unwilling to spend the time necessary to help students develop these characteristics and skills. We understand the time required for class meetings and the demands placed on school personnel who have limited time to devote to what they consider "nonacademic" activities. But the benefits to both students and teachers are well worth the time and training it takes to learn effective class-meeting skills.

Some classroom teachers are reluctant to start one more new thing. Others think they will be giving up too much control. Teachers who think class meetings take too much time away from academic learning forget how much time they waste every day handling discipline problems that could be handled more effectively in a class meeting. We talked with a fourth-grade teacher who had all these objections. She said,

> When our school psychologist gave me a copy of *Positive Discipline* and wanted me to implement class meetings, my initial reaction was, "Oh, no. This is another program that I'm going to have to read and it's not going to work." No one could have a more negative attitude to this than I did, but I decided to try it anyway. After one week I was sold.

This teacher also admitted that she gained more control than she lost when classroom control became the responsibility of everyone in the class. Before she implemented class meetings, she was in the psychologist's office several times a week seeking help for dealing with her many problem students. She seldom seeks the advice of the psychologist anymore. She and her students are solving problems and helping each other.

We cannot sufficiently stress the importance of student participation in the problem-solving process to create cooperation, collaboration, positive motivation, and healthy self-esteem. How could this not improve the academic climate? Class meetings provide a solid base for the teaching, retention, and positive application of academic learning. Understanding this basic fact requires an understanding of long-range results instead of short-term convenience.

The Big Picture

All too often, school administrators and teachers do not see the big picture for young people. They overlook the crucial need for the development of life skills. They rely (often futilely) on external control through punishments and rewards instead of taking the time and energy to help students learn control from within through dialogue and problem solving. Teachers often choose a punishment/ reward system (external controls) because they believe that it teaches children responsibility. However, this system actually makes the *teacher* responsible, not the students. It is the teacher's responsibility to catch students being *good* and reward them, or catch them being *bad* and punish them. What happens when the teacher is not around?

Another illusion perpetuated by the external-control system is that it works. It is true that punishment will usually stop misbehavior for a while, and rewards will often serve as motivators. However, sometimes we must "beware of what works." It is important to consider more than the short-term results of external control and ask, "What are the positive long-range results?" Extensive research[5] has shown that punishment and rewards have many long-term negative results (such as rebellion, the negative use of power, or thoughtless compliance) and do not teach self-

---

5. Alphie Kohn, *Punished by Rewards* (New York: Houghton Mifflin, 1993).

discipline, self-control, or any other important character-istics and skills for success in life.

What About Other Influences?

We often hear this question from teachers: "What can I do when the student has such a terrible home life?" The answer is, "A lot." Young people have several major influences in their lives: home, school, peer group, and (sometimes) church. Teachers cannot do anything directly about the home or church lives of students, but they can have a direct, positive impact on school and peer group experiences, which constitute a large portion of a student's day. The skills and attitudes learned by students have a ripple effect on the playground, the community, and the home. Certainly it would be easier if homes and schools were working together. However, giving students some exposure to positive life skills is much better than giving up because they experience a negative home environment.

One of the sad circumstances of teaching is that too often teachers never see the fruits of their labor. They plant the seeds but don't experience the harvest. One of the benefits of class meetings is that the teacher does not have to do all the labor and planting alone.

Teachers do not have to feel overwhelmed by the responsibility of their power to nurture and influence students. Through class meetings, students learn to help one another. Everyone benefits. Responsible citizenship requires a high degree of social interest—the desire and ability to contribute in socially useful ways and not to participate in antisocial behavior. In class meetings, students solve problems together and learn the tools of mutual respect, cooperation, and collaboration. They experience positive power, and this empowerment reduces their need to act out and create discipline problems in order to feel powerful.

Putting It All Together

The following puzzle provides an overview of the components of *Positive Discipline in the Classroom*. As you can see, class meetings are only one of the components of the puzzle. Although each of these components is covered in upcoming chapters, two of them are prevailing themes in every chapter: creating an atmosphere of caring based on kindness and firmness, dignity and mutual respect, and using Positive Discipline classroom management tools. Each time we introduce one of the parts of the Positive Discipline puzzle, we'll show its accompanying graphic. All of the strategies that are taught for effective class meetings also can be used throughout the school day. It is important to remember that it takes all of the puzzle pieces to make a complete picture of an effective Positive Discipline in the Classroom program.

Teachers who wish to replace authoritarian methods with democratic ones will focus on long-range results instead of short-term convenience. When teachers have faith in themselves and their students and are willing to believe that skills can be learned, successful class meetings will likely result. Positive Discipline methods are effective when teachers are willing to give up control over students in favor of working with students in a cooperative manner. Teachers who learn how to ask more questions and give fewer lectures develop a real curiosity about their students' thoughts and opinions. When kids are encouraged to express their opinions, are given choices instead of edicts, and can use group problem solving, the classroom atmosphere improves as it becomes one of cooperation, collaboration, and mutual respect. The dream can become a reality.

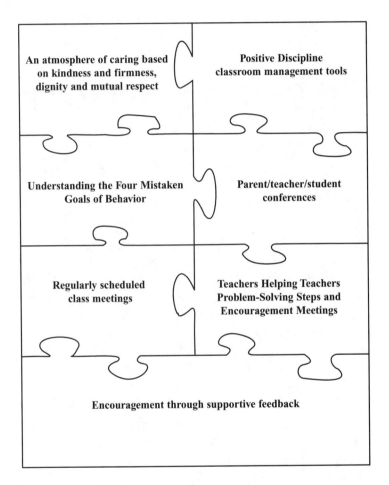

▼

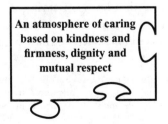

Chapter

2

The Message of Caring

Paradise could be attained if man knew how to apply his knowledge for the benefit of all.

Rudolf Dreikurs

We have established that Positive Discipline in the Classroom is based on a foundation of mutual respect. Creating an atmosphere of caring (kindness and firmness at the same time) is the first piece of the Positive Discipline puzzle, and putting it in place insures that the foundation isn't built on sand.

An atmosphere of caring based on kindness and firmness, dignity and mutual respect

A group of middle school students were asked, "What usually happens when you get in trouble at school?" The kids responded with various answers, including detention, Saturday school, lunch detention, suspension, extra homework, getting yelled at, being grounded or beaten at home, having parents come to school and sit with them to embarrass them, or referral (which they defined as getting sent to the office to listen to a speech).

They were then asked, "How many of you have experienced any of these consequences?" Two out of ten had been beaten at home for poor behavior in school. Five had had their parents come to school. Every one had served detention, been grounded, been yelled at, or received extra homework. At least seven out of ten had received lunch detention, Saturday school, and suspension. When asked if these interventions helped them do better in school, they said "No!" in unison. When asked if these interventions helped them feel loved, cared for, and motivated to cooperate, the students laughed and replied, "What do you think?"

"Why do you think grown-ups do these kinds of things if they don't help?" we continued. "Because they like the power," some answered. "You don't think they do it because they care about you and want to help you do better?" we asked. The kids just laughed.

Dr. James Tunney, a former educator and NFL referee, did a study for his doctoral dissertation to measure levels of perceived caring.[1] He first surveyed principals with the question, "Do you care about your teachers?" The principals always reported high levels of caring. Dr. Tunney then surveyed the teachers and found that they perceived extremely low levels of caring from their principals.

---

1. James Joseph Tunney and James Mancel Jenkins, "A Comparison of Climate as Perceived by Selected Students, Faculty and Administrators in PASCL, Innovative and Other High Schools" (Ph.D. diss., University of Southern California, 1975).

The next step was to ask the teachers, "Do you care about your students?" Of course, the teachers reported high levels of caring about the students. But guess what? The students perceived extremely low levels of caring from their teachers.

During in-service training when we ask teachers how many of them care about kids, just about every hand goes up. Then we ask how many think the kids know they care, and though fewer hands are raised, most teachers still believe students are getting the message. Unfortunately, as Dr. Tunney's research shows, very few kids believe teachers care about them unless they are A students who have "psyched out the teacher" and know how to play the teacher's game.

Kids know you care when you find out who they are, encourage them to see mistakes as opportunities to learn and grow, and have faith in their ability to make a meaningful contribution. They know you care when they feel that they are listened to and that their thoughts and feelings are taken seriously. They know you care when you respect them enough to involve them in decision-making processes. They know you care when you help them understand the consequences of their choices in a non-threatening environment that encourages problem solving instead of punishment. All these things happen during class meetings, with a minimum investment in patience and time for skill building. An atmosphere of caring begins with the teacher who guides students to treat one another in ways that demonstrate caring.

The Power of Caring

Carter Bayton, a teacher in an inner-city New York school, expressed the idea of caring in these moving words: "You have to reach the heart before you can reach the mind."

In September 1991, *Life* magazine featured a story about Bayton and seventeen second graders who had been labeled "unteachable" in a regular classroom. He taught them so well that in six months they challenged the "regular class" (which they had been deemed unfit to enter) to a math contest—and won!

Carter Bayton understands the importance of treating students with kindness and firmness. He knows it's important to make sure the message of caring gets through. This is a truly essential part of a teacher-student relationship. We have many opportunities to convey our message of caring, and we must be sure to seize them. When students feel cared about, they want to cooperate, not misbehave. When they do not need to misbehave to gain attention and significance, they are free to learn. Positive Discipline methods provide a format in which students can gain attention and feel significant and productive.

Barriers and Builders

Respect and encouragement are two basic ingredients of caring. We have identified five common behaviors (barriers) that adults use with young people that are disrespectful and discouraging, and five behaviors (builders) that are respectful and encouraging.[2]

Barrier 1: Assuming

We often assume we know what students think and feel without asking them. We also assume what they can or

2. See also H. Stephen Glenn and Jane Nelsen, *Raising Self-Reliant Children in a Self-Indulgent World* (Rocklin, Calif.: Prima, 1989); *Empowering Others: Ten Keys to Affirming and Validating People*, a video with H. Stephen Glenn (Orem, Utah: Empowering People Books, Tapes, and Videos, 1988), 1-800-456-7770; and the Developing Capable People Course by H. Stephen Glenn, (916) 338-6662.

can't do and how they should or shouldn't respond. We then deal with them according to our assumptions, preventing us from discovering their unique perceptions and capabilities.

Builder 1: Checking

Positive Discipline methods provide an opportunity for teachers to discover what students actually think and feel. When we check instead of assume, we discover how students are maturing in their ability to deal with problems and issues that affect them.

One special-education teacher trained in behavior modification assumed her students were not capable of participating in class meetings; she believed it was her job to control their behavior. She was encouraged to test her assumptions by trying a class meeting. Even though the children couldn't write their names, each had a special "mark" they could stamp on the agenda to signify they wanted help with a problem. The teacher discovered that the children were more capable than she assumed. They quickly learned to express their needs at the class meeting and engaged in problem solving far beyond the teacher's assumptions.

Barrier 2: Rescuing/Explaining

We often think we are being caring or helpful when we do things for students rather than allow them to learn from their own experiences. Likewise, we may think we're being helpful by explaining things to students instead of letting them discover the explanation for themselves. You might find it interesting to tally the number of times you rescue students while giving them a lecture, explaining what happened, what caused it to happen, how they should feel about it, and what they should do. For example, a teacher might take a child by the hand and find his

21

or her coat for him or her while delivering a lecture on responsibility. You might also find it interesting to observe the blank look on a student's face to see if, by any chance, he or she is as interested in the lecture as you are.

Builder 2: Exploring

Teachers explain and rescue when they say, "It's cold outside, so don't forget your jackets." Teachers explore when they say, "As you look outside, what do you need to think about before you go out to recess? What do you need to do to take care of yourselves?" For the student who can't find his jacket, help him explore the situation by asking, "What ideas do you have to solve this problem?"

Positive Discipline methods enable teachers and students to help each other learn to make choices as well as understand themselves, others, and situations through their own experiences. It is part of the class-meeting process for students to explore what happened, what caused it to happen, how behavior affects others and how they feel about it, and what they can do to solve the problem. If you pay close attention, you will notice that students come to the same conclusions from their own wisdom that they seem to ignore when given to them through adult lectures. This kind of exploration helps students develop an internal locus of control instead of an external locus of control.

Barrier 3: Directing

We don't realize how disrespectful we are to students when we direct them: "Pick that up! Put that away! Straighten up your desk before the bell rings!" These are all directives that reinforce dependency, eliminate initiative and cooperation, and encourage passive-aggressive behavior (grudgingly doing the minimum amount of work and leaving as much undone as possible in order to "bug" the teacher).

Builder 3: Inviting/Encouraging

Positive Discipline methods allow teachers to involve students in the planning and problem-solving activities that can help them become self-directed: "The bell will ring soon. I would appreciate anything any of you could do to help me get the room straightened up for the next class." Directing invites passive or active resistance and/or rebellion. Inviting encourages cooperation.

Barrier 4: Expecting

It is important that teachers have high expectations for young people and believe in their potential. However, when that potential becomes the standard and we judge them for falling short, we discourage them: "I was expecting more maturity from you. I thought you were more responsible than that. I expected you to be the kind of student your brother was."

Builder 4: Celebrating

Class meetings let teachers and students acknowledge each other through compliments and problem solving. When we are quick to celebrate any movement in the direction of a student's potential or maturity, we encourage. When we demand too much too soon, we discourage.

A student who has never risked asking a question and who suddenly asks a question unrelated to the topic being discussed could be affirmed for asking the question instead of criticized for not paying attention. This student could then be asked if he or she has anything to say about the topic being discussed. Students who cheat can be affirmed for their desire to get a better grade and then be invited to explore other ways to accomplish their goal.

Barrier 5: "Adultisms"

"Adultisms" occur when we forget that children are not mature adults and expect them to think and act like adults. Examples of the language of "ism-ing" are, "How come you never _____? Why can't you ever _____? Surely you realize _____? How many times do I have to tell you? I can't believe you would do such a thing! You are such a disappointment." Almost anything that begins with the words *should* or *ought* or with an angry tone of voice is usually an adultism. Adultisms produce guilt and shame rather than support and encouragement. The message of an "ism" is, "Since you don't see what I see, you are at fault."

Builder 5: Respecting

Positive Discipline methods encourage interaction between teachers and students that help both understand differences in how people perceive things. This understanding creates a climate of acceptance that encourages growth and effective communication. Instead of judging people for what they don't see, we encourage them to seek understanding of themselves and others. Instead of saying, "You knew what I wanted on this project!" a teacher could say, "What is your understanding of the requirements for this project?" or "What were you thinking of when you presented your project this way?"

An important factor is that students often don't have the same priorities as adults. Math and science or school in general may not be in students' top-one-hundred list of priorities. This does not mean that they should not be required to study math and science. It does mean that it is respectful for teachers to understand that students may have other priorities such as friends (or not having any), sports (or not being chosen for the team), cars ("Will I ever be able to afford one?"), sleeping in ("Doesn't my teacher know I'm on a different time clock?"), or good or bad family relationships. The list goes on and on. It is important for teachers to understand the life issues and priorities of their students instead of ignoring them. Class meetings provide an opportunity for students to explore and resolve many of the life issues that are troubling to them. Teachers can then use some of these issues and priorities to help students explore the relevance of learning in order to invite them to cooperate instead of to resist and rebel.

The five barriers discourage students from growing and developing into capable young people. Teachers who use the barriers usually have good intentions; they believe students will be motivated by assumptions, by being rescued and directed, by expectations, and by "isms." But the barriers create frustration and discouragement for teachers and students alike. Switching to the five builders empowers both teachers and students. As teachers think of students as people, it is easier to empower students by checking, exploring, inviting and encouraging, celebrating, and respecting. A teacher tells the following story.

> When I first heard about the barriers and builders, I realized that I was using barriers with my students. I assumed they needed me to step in and take care of things, explain things, direct them where to go and what to do, point out where they fell short of my expectations for the day by "shoulding" on them. Then I ended up lecturing, using expressions such as "How many times must I tell you?" or "You know better than that!" I felt exhausted, and the students weren't progressing.
>
> I switched to builders. I checked the students' understanding of a problem, explored their perceptions

of how to work with it, invited their assistance in finding a solution, celebrated any movement in the desired direction rather than pointing out where they fell short of my expectations, and showed respect for them by honoring their thoughts and feelings. The classroom atmosphere improved; so did my disposition and the kids' progress.

We guarantee one hundred percent improvement in student-teacher relationships when teachers simply learn to recognize barrier behaviors and stop demonstrating them. Where else can you get such a generous return for ceasing a behavior? And when the builders are added, the payoff is even greater.

A high school principal told us that the chapter on barriers and builders in *Raising Self-Reliant Children in a Self-Indulgent World* totally changed his relationship with his twenty-two-year-old daughter who was away at college. The next time he had a telephone conversation with her, he listened. Every time he felt tempted to use his usual barriers of expecting, assuming, lecturing, rescuing, or directing, he kept his mouth shut. His daughter opened up and told him more than she ever had before. At the end of the conversation, she said, "You sure are different, Dad." She called more often after that, and there was a warmer feeling between them. He concluded his story by saying, "You were right. I got one hundred percent return in an improved relationship by doing nothing."

Caring Attitudes and Skills

In addition to the barriers and builders, there are attitude changes teachers can make and skills they can learn that will demonstrate to students that their teachers really care about them.

26

Being Aware of Tone of Voice

Many teachers are completely unaware of their tone of voice and how it can affect students. In one junior high school class, for example, the students were in serious conflict with their teacher, who couldn't understand their hostility. A visitor to the classroom was shocked to watch the teacher's manner and listen to her tone of voice. Whenever students misbehaved, she yelled at them, criticized them, and humiliated them in front of their classmates. After class the visitor asked the teacher if she would like some feedback. She said yes and was told, "You are trying to put out a small fire with a blowtorch." Having been completely unaware of her manner and tone, the teacher changed both by the next class period. That same day she told another faculty member, "My classes have been much smoother this afternoon since I decided to put away my blowtorch."

During a Positive Discipline in the Classroom workshop, one teacher was amazed as she realized, "When I criticize my students, I say it loud enough for others to hear. When I have something nice to say, it is in a soft voice that others usually don't hear."

Listening and Taking Kids Seriously

A seventeen-year-old high school student decided not to turn in any of his homework in order to punish his teacher for her "attitude problem." Whenever he tried to talk to her about homework, he thought she was insinuating that he was lazy and that she didn't take him seriously. He did well on the tests, and he thought the teacher was picking on him because he didn't turn in his work.

With encouragement from his parents, he decided to talk to his teacher about his feelings. This time she really listened. When he finished, she said, "I know it seems unfair that I insist on homework regardless of how well you do on a test. I'm sorry this upsets you, but I'm unwilling to change the rule. I thought you didn't care about school, and I apologize for treating you disrespectfully. I'm glad you took the time to tell me how you feel." Although the conversation didn't change the homework situation, the young man felt understood and accepted, and he stopped acting out in the classroom.

Enjoying the Job

Robert Rasmussen, called Ras by his students, was voted High School Teacher of the Year five years in a row by juniors and seniors. The school district also honored him as Teacher of the Year.

While Ras was out of the room, we asked the students why they thought he received these honors. Their answers could be divided into three categories: (1) he respects us, (2) he listens to us, and (3) he enjoys his job. "What does enjoying the job have to do with anything?" we asked. One of the students explained, "Many teachers come to work with an attitude problem. They hate us. They hate their jobs. They seem to hate life. They take it out on us. Ras is always up. He seems to enjoy us, his job, and life in general."

Ras has a unique way of making sure the message of caring gets through. He has a teddy bear in his classroom. He introduces the bear to his students and says, "This is our care bear. If any of you feels discouraged or a little down, come get the bear. He'll make you feel better." At first the students think he's bonkers. After all, they are high school juniors and seniors, young adults. But it doesn't take long for them to catch the spirit. Every day several students, including the big football players, go to Ras's desk and say, "I need the bear."

The bear concept became so popular that Ras had to provide more bears to keep up with the demand. Sometimes the kids carry them around all day, but they always bring them back. Sometimes, when Ras sees a student who looks a little down, he tosses a bear to the student. This is his symbolic way of saying, "I care. I don't have time to spend with you personally right now, but I care."

Appreciating Uniqueness

A student thinks a teacher cares when his or her uniqueness is recognized. One teacher made a set of baseball cards for his third-grade class, with each card featuring a student's picture and nickname. The nicknames expressed the unique interest of each child. For example, one card said, "Cat-Lover Colleen," and another, "Home-Run Sean." Although it takes time and skill to make a set of baseball cards, it can be fun to let the kids come up with nicknames together, as long as the activity remains respectful.

Another way of expressing each student's uniqueness is to have them create their own T-shirts. Give each student a piece of paper cut out in the form of a T-shirt, with the following instructions:

1. Write your name at the top of the shirt.
2. In the middle, write one word that describes you.
3. Write words that describe some of your characteristics and special interests all over the shirt.
4. Across the bottom, write one thing about you that most people probably don't know.
5. Tape the T-shirt on your clothes with masking tape, and walk around the room. Talk to at least three other people using the information on your T-shirt as the basis of conversation.

Developing an Appropriate Attitude

Think about how you feel when you're watching babies and toddlers; it seems like everything they do is adorable.

See if you can get to the point with your students where you can truly say, "Aren't they adorable!"

When we are able to see behavior as age appropriate, it helps us see otherwise annoying behavior as adorable (or at least interesting). A third-grade boy in torn, dirty pants will begin to look adorable; a seventh-grader acting like a "big shot" will bring a smile; and you might even look forward to hearing the latest installment from a high school student who "knows much more than you."

Having a Sense of Humor

Sometimes teachers forget to see the humor in situations with students. It's okay not to be serious all the time. Mrs. Turner plays a game called Let's Make a Deal with her class, and the kids love it. She says, "Okay kids, it's time for Let's Make a Deal. I like to start on time, and you like to leave on time. I'll save up the time I have to wait to get started, and you can make it up after school. Deal?" The kids groan and then settle down.

Mr. Barkley has a droll sense of humor that kids love. They know he cares about them and whether or not they succeed in school. Some teachers use sarcasm in the guise of humor to put students down, and others may "go for a laugh" at a student's expense. With Mr. Barkley the students sense the feeling behind what he does, and his caring comes through. If there is sincere caring for the kids, they will get the message.

One day Mr. Barkley was dealing with a daydreaming student. He put his hand lightly on the boy's shoulder and said, "Picture this. You're eighteen years old. You get up and turn on MTV. You know everyone on the videos and all the words to the songs. But will anyone give you a job? No way! And why not? Because you spent all your time in my class staring into space." The student looked up, grinned, and opened his book.

Later in the period a student, Jennifer, was passing notes to a friend and paying no attention to a play Mr. Barkley was reading to the class. In a smooth but slightly louder voice, Mr. Barkley read, "To be or not to be, that is the question Jennifer asks herself each day." She looked up and said, "Huh? Were you calling on me?" Mr. Barkley said, "Did anyone hear me call on Jennifer? I don't think so." Jennifer paid attention to the rest of class.

Respecting Students' Outside Interests

It's easy to forget that students have other interests in life besides school. Their social life is extremely important to them, and often they are dealing with issues of rejection or popularity. They may be dealing with the trauma of not being chosen for teams or never being the first or the best. By the time they reach junior high and high school, they may have job issues, car issues, dating issues, sex issues, and drug issues. Many kids operate according to a different clock than adults do. They like to stay up late and then have difficulty getting up in the morning. Yet they have to conform to an early start at school.

We saw this note pasted on a door of a high school classroom in Charlotte, North Carolina: "Tardies, please come into the room quietly, find a seat, look for your directions on the board. Learning begins as soon as the tardy bell rings." Instead of humiliating or punishing latecomers, this teacher respectfully allows students to experience the consequences and take care of what they need to do to catch up. Students can come in and start working right away instead of going to the office, getting papers, feeling like they're in trouble, and disturbing the class.

Another teacher tells his students, "I won't take roll until five minutes after the tardy bell. I know some of you have jobs and have a difficult time handling all the demands of being a teenager. It would be better if you could sleep in until 10:00, go to school until 5:00, and have the rest of the evening for family time, jobs, and a social life." The kids cheer. They do their best not to take advantage. They respect this teacher because they feel respected. He knows how to make sure the message of caring gets through.

Respect invites respect. Disrespect invites disrespect. When students are acting disrespectfully, teachers might take a look a their own behavior.

Involving Students

Many teachers are used to directing students and trying to solve student problems themselves. Then they wonder why students resist. We have been in many classrooms where the teacher's neatly printed "Classroom Rules" are posted on the wall. With this method, students become passive recipients of a teacher's demands—what an invitation for them to either give in or rebel.

Some teachers have found a way to invite cooperation. On the first day of school they ask the kids to help brainstorm classroom rules. Their list of ideas is quickly scribbled on paper, labeled "Our Rules," and posted on the wall. This is an invitation for kids to cooperate because they have participated in the decisions. What is surprising is that the rules are the same as, or stricter than, the rules teachers try to force on students.

Creating a classroom job list is another effective and fun way to involve students and let them know each is special and needed. (See chapter 11 for detailed information on how to do this.)

Students feel a teacher's caring when they are consulted and involved. They rise to the occasion when a teacher says, "This is our learning environment, and together we are responsible for making it work." Teachers who fear a loss of control if they allow that kind of student input will be delighted to find that control is not needed. Cooperation and collaboration, based on mutual respect, replace control.

Improvement, Not Perfection

Students know a teacher cares when the teacher encourages improvement instead of insisting on perfection. The class-meeting process provides an excellent opportunity for students to trust this philosophy. Class meetings may never be perfect, but every failure can provide an opportunity for solutions. The teacher should continue asking, "What can we do to solve this problem?" Not only does this question show that the teacher cares, it encourages kids to care about each other.

Positive Discipline methods help create the kind of environment for empowering students to be respectful, resourceful, cooperative, and capable—one step at a time. It is worth the effort.

Caring in Class Meetings

The power of caring through class meetings is demonstrated in the following examples. Frank Meder, a teacher in the Sacramento City School District, started class meetings in a school where violence in the elementary school was so bad that the janitor periodically had to clean up blood. Vandalism was so prevalent that the sheriff was called on a weekly basis. Frank said that he got a stomachache every Sunday afternoon around 1:00 because he dreaded returning to the classroom Monday morning. When Frank decided to try class meetings, he felt more desperate than hopeful. He doubted that his disruptive students could learn cooperation and problem-solving skills; he was delighted to be proven wrong. The year Frank started class meetings, it came to the attention of his principal that although there were sixty-one suspensions for fights, not one student was from Frank's class. She also noticed that Frank's students came to school more regularly and were improving academically. When the principal sat in on one of Frank's class meetings, she realized what a great preventive tool the meeting was and asked Frank to show all the teachers in the school how to conduct class meetings.

The following year every teacher, first through sixth grade, held class meetings at least four times a week. The following statistics were reported by Ann Platt in her master's thesis at California State University, Sacramento: only four suspensions for fighting as opposed to sixty-one the year before; only two cases of reported vandalism, as opposed to twenty-four the year before.[3]

In another instance, a school with a serious graffiti problem kept hiring painters to repaint the walls. Every time a wall was repainted, the kids put graffiti on it again. One of the teachers suggested asking the student body for ideas on how to solve the problem. The students decreed that when kids were caught writing on the wall, they would be supervised by another student while they repainted. It's no surprise that the graffiti problem disappeared.

Another example of the power of caring through a class meeting is provided by Earl Lesk.[4] Mr. Lesk, a high school teacher, decided to initiate regular class meetings in his Biology 11 and 12 classes. He asked his students if

---

3. Ann Roeder Platt, "Efficacy of Class Meetings in Elementary Schools" (master's thesis, California State University, 1979).
4. Earl Lesk, "Freedom with Responsibility," *The B.C. Teacher*, January/February 1982.

they would like to participate, and they said yes. One eleventh-grade student, who'd had difficulty in all aspects of the course but finished the semester successfully, summed up the class's feelings: "By using encouragement and by not forcing people to do things, the class became more independent and cooperative, which allowed us to use our own initiative to put forth a good effort."

These teachers and schools have incorporated class meetings with excellent results. They are just a few of the many who have experienced tremendous success by starting class meetings. If a teacher is willing to learn a process that teaches students many valuable skills, it can also make the job easier and more fun. Helping students experience caring, belonging, and significance is the most powerful thing a teacher can do, motivating them to fulfill their highest potential—academically and otherwise.

Effective Positive Discipline methods help students become more self-confident. They help improve self-esteem by increasing a sense of belonging and self-acceptance. As students contribute and participate in a Positive Discipline classroom, they find that they have the ability to make a difference and feel a sense of ownership through involvement. Putting the first piece of the Positive Discipline puzzle in place makes it easy for students to understand that teachers care about them and their concerns and that their contributions are valued.

Chapter

3

Building Blocks for Effective Class Meetings

No problem is too difficult once it is recognized as a common task.

Rudolf Dreikurs

Not all types of class meetings are the same. There are many types of student-teacher meetings. Positive Discipline class meetings are different from other methods because they are effective only when they are perceived as an ongoing process that is designed to teach students many life skills that are as important as academics. Class meetings are not meant to be used once in awhile to solve a crisis. It takes time to create an atmosphere of caring, communication skills, and mutual respect. It takes time for students and teachers to learn the benefits of focusing on solutions instead of punishment. Without regularly scheduled class meetings, students don't develop the skills for success in solving problems. That is why we consider holding regularly scheduled class meetings another part of the Positive Discipline puzzle as discussed in chapters 4 through 10.

In Positive Discipline class meetings, the teacher does not determine the topics to be discussed and does not do most of the talking (preaching, lecturing) in an effort to manipulate students into good behavior. Students usually resist and tune out teacher-dominated meetings. The Positive Discipline class meeting is a process that involves teachers and students in true dialogue and problem solving on issues of real and practical concern to everyone. Most of the agenda items are student-initiated, although we suggest teachers also put their concerns on the agenda so that students can help solve some of the teacher's problems. When students and teachers collaborate, they learn to appreciate each other, to understand and respect differences, and to develop social interest.

Social Interest

Social interest is one of the most important life skills students can learn. Actually, social interest is more than a skill. It is *Gemeinschaftsgefühl*. Gemeinschaftsgefühl is a German word that was coined by Alfred Adler.[1] It is difficult to translate into English because it means so much: an attitude of caring and concern for others, for the community, and for the environment—and the action required to demonstrate this concern. The closest Adler could come to an English translation is "social interest."

People are not born with social interest. It takes education, training, and practice. Positive Discipline class meetings offer a process in which students can develop this important life attitude and the skills to accomplish true social interest.

Feedback and Training

After hearing about the many benefits of class meetings, many teachers try them, only to be discouraged by poor results. If you are one of those teachers, we encourage you to read this entire book before you decide "never again." You may discover the reasons for previous problems and the skills for success.

A fourth-grade teacher was struggling with a group of students who had driven previous teachers to tranquilizers and fantasies of early retirement. He hoped class meetings would be the way to teach his students cooperation and responsibility. After trying and failing, he discovered that holding class meetings once a week with the students remaining in rows at their desks was the problem. Shortly after he started holding the meetings in a circle format for twenty minutes every day, his class changed dramatically.

---

1. Many of the concepts in this book are based on the teachings of Alfred Adler, M.D., and Rudolf Dreikurs, M.D. Both were psychiatrists who taught democratic processes to parents and teachers in Vienna, Austria, and other countries before bringing their philosophy to the United States.

Several teachers have found that their class meetings felt like kangaroo courts until they made two very important changes: they started focusing on solutions instead of consequences, and they allowed the students with the problems to choose the brainstormed suggestions that would help them the most instead of allowing the whole class to determine their fate.

After receiving training in Positive Discipline in the Classroom, some teachers discover they have been patronizing, punitive, and controlling, or they have allowed humiliation to take place in their classes. Class meetings will not be successful under these conditions. Many teachers have discovered that making some small change in what they have been doing is enough to bring a positive atmosphere to their class meeting process. Six of their most important discoveries, each of which is discussed in more detail in later chapters, are summarized below.

Six Criteria for Successful Class Meetings

1. Have class meetings every day. It is better to have a ten- to twenty-minute class meeting every day than a thirty- to forty-five-minute class meeting once a week. (We know this is difficult for middle and high school teachers to accept. Later we will discuss how it can be done without sacrificing academic learning time.)

2. Form a circle. Take the time and training that is required for students to move their desks out of the way and put their chairs into a circle. Once students learn the routine, this usually takes less than one minute. Some teachers prefer to have their students sit in a circle on the floor when space allows.

3. Focus on solutions instead of consequences. Too many students and teachers still use punishment, and focusing on solutions helps eliminate this problem.

4. Pass an item (such as a special stick, which can be called the "talking stick," or a stuffed animal) around the circle. Students take their turn to speak or pass only when they have the item in their hand. This provides order and encourages every student (including shy students who may not bother to raise their hands) the opportunity to speak or pass.

5. Allow the student who put the problem on the agenda to choose the solution he or she thinks will be helpful, and/or allow the student who is "the focus" of the problem to choose a solution instead of allowing the students to vote. This increases the feeling of empowerment and accountability for students.

6. Allow time for training while teachers and students learn the class-meeting process—often through mistakes. This can take as long as twenty-one days. Trust the process.

It takes time for teachers and students to give up control and punishment and become comfortable with new methods. Most of us are willing to take the time for training when we see the value of new methods. Teacher commitment to the class-meeting process is actually the most important factor in successful class meetings. Teachers who understand that life skills are as important as academic skills are willing to take the time and to teach the skills for effective class meetings.

Eight Building Blocks for Effective Class Meetings

Training in the Eight Building Blocks is the surest route to success. Proficiency in each of these building-block skill areas will produce meetings in which kids want to become involved in social interest and the problem-solving process. It takes about two hours to introduce these concepts to students. Instead of doing it all at once, we recommend that you hold short sessions and take at least four class meetings to cover the basics, which are discussed in this book in chapters 3 through 7. Let your students know that you are taking extra time in the beginning to lay the groundwork for successful class meetings. If the topics are introduced gradually, students will be less restless and will have a chance to practice the skills they have learned. The Eight Building Blocks are listed below.

1. Form a circle.
2. Practice compliments and appreciation.
3. Create an agenda.
4. Develop communication skills.
5. Learn about separate realities.
6. Recognize the four reasons people do what they do.
7. Practice role playing and brainstorming.
8. Focus on nonpunitive solutions.

Getting Agreement First

Before forming your first circle and beginning to introduce the Eight Building Blocks to your class, take time to introduce the idea of class meetings to your students and get their "buy in." We have found that the following discussions work well with various age groups.

Introduce your students to the idea that you would like to begin holding class meetings in which they can express their concerns and use their power and skills to help make decisions. Elementary students are usually eager to try class meetings. Simply ask for a show of hands of how many students would like to begin. When teachers use the attitudes and skills we have discussed, elementary students rarely resist.

With junior high and high school students, however, it is helpful to get them to buy in to the idea of class meetings before starting; otherwise, they may resist and may sabotage the process. Using language appropriate for your grade level, initiate a discussion about power. Talk to them about how problems are usually handled in your school (with punishment and reward). Point out how that method creates a one-up/one-down system in which adults tell kids what to do and kids either comply or rebel without thinking or without becoming involved. It is a win-lose system. None of us want to be the loser, so we need to create a win-win system.

To encourage discussion, ask questions such as these: "Who has an example they would like to share about what happens when someone tries to control you? What do you feel? What do you do? What do you learn? How do you try to control or manipulate others, including teachers?" Kids will usually say that they feel angry or scared and manipulated. What they learn is to rebel or comply. Compliance may seem like a good thing on the surface, but it is very detrimental when we consider the loss of confidence and self-esteem that is the basis of compliance in a controlling environment. Cooperation is much better than compliance and occurs in an environment of mutual respect in which people work together for win-win solutions.

Ask your students if they would like to be more involved in the decisions that affect their lives. Would they be willing to do the work required to come up with win-win solutions? Point out that some students actually prefer having adults boss them around so that they can rebel. Other students like having adults direct them so that they don't have to take responsibility themselves. It takes more time and personal responsibility from everyone to use class meetings effectively. Make it clear that you would prefer to work with the class to learn a respectful method of working together, but if the students aren't ready, you would be happy to make the rules yourself and invite the students to try again at regularly scheduled intervals to be involved and work with you. This kind of discussion is especially helpful and effective in classrooms in which students have been taught with authoritarian methods.

Another possibility is to start a discussion by asking your students how many have family meetings at home. Ask what happens at family meetings. Let them know that class meetings are a place where they can help each other, share ideas, solve problems, and plan things together. Mention that while it's okay to discuss anything at a class meeting that happens at school, there may be some items that can't be changed, like curriculum or school policies. Nevertheless, if someone has a concern about these matters, it can be discussed with the intention of determining the best way to deal with things that can't be changed.

Daily Class Meetings

Once you have the interest and go-ahead of your students, inform the group how often you will be holding class meetings so that everyone will know ahead of time. As discussed above, it is better to have short meetings once a day than longer meetings once a week. Students cannot learn and retain the process when they experience it only once a week.

At a workshop, teachers were asked if they would teach math only once a week. They said, "Of course not." When asked why, they replied, "Because they couldn't learn and have enough practice by once-a-week exposure." This is equally true for important life skills. Also, if meetings are held only once a week, younger students might be discouraged from putting something on an agenda that already has ten items. Because they know only three or four topics can be covered in a single meeting, they may be frustrated at having to wait three to four weeks before their concerns are addressed. Once a week may be enough for older students and students with strong problem-solving skills. However, once teachers experience the benefit to their students, they find the process so valuable for teaching cooperation and life skills that they hold class meetings daily.

Middle schools and high schools that have made a commitment to the class-meeting process have found creative ways to allow students to have this experience daily. Some have twenty-five-minute advisory periods in the morning and use this time for class meetings. Other schools have chosen to alternate class meetings in different subject departments. For example, math teachers will have class meetings on Mondays, English teachers on Tuesdays, science teachers on Wednesdays, and so forth. One high school teacher could not convince any of her colleagues to try class meetings, but she remained committed to the idea. Her class period was only forty-five-minutes long. She held class meetings that lasted ten minutes of every period and rotated the format. On Mondays and Fridays the students would go around the circle giving acknowledgments and appreciations. Tuesdays they would practice one of the activities (described in later chapters) to increase their skills in the Eight Building Blocks for Effective Class Meetings. Wednesdays and Thursdays were problem-solving days. Sometimes they would spend two days discussing one problem. Other weeks they found they could get through more than one problem in the ten-minute time allotted. All of these teachers find that academic learning is enhanced by the atmosphere of respect and cooperation created by class meetings. For this reason they don't feel the time spent on class meetings takes away from subject matter.

A high school math teacher has daily meetings with his basic math students and weekly meetings with his pre-calculus seniors. The meetings last ten to fifteen minutes, although he allowed twenty minutes at the beginning of the year to go over class-meeting procedures. He schedules them at the end of the period because the students often get so involved, the meetings would cut into his lesson plan if he started them at the beginning of the period. Although he was concerned that class meetings would take away from academic learning, he found that his students now do better academically. He said, "Either the class meetings are extremely effective, or kids are getting smarter these days. My students resisted when I first started class meetings. Now they don't let me forget them."

Once a Week Is the Best I Can Do

We've talked to counselors in different schools who have been introducing the idea of class meetings to their faculty. They say that for starters, the best they can expect teachers to go along with is a class meeting once a week. They also commented that the success of the meeting is more dependent on the atmosphere created by the teacher than the age of the students.

As students get older, they're able to retain class-meeting skills for a longer period of time. For this reason it can be effective to have class meetings only once a week if longer blocks of time are not possible. Even though older students are able to wait longer than elementary school students, the opportunity to present their concerns and work on solutions at least once a week is important. When teachers start meeting once a week and experience some success, they often want to meet for shorter times more often.

It is important for teachers to decide not only how often to hold meetings but also the time of day that is best for them. We suggest you hold meetings just before a natural stopping time, such as lunch. Students often don't want to stop class meetings if a less enjoyable subject follows. However, they will stop for lunch.

Introduce your students to the format for class meetings so that they know what will happen in the meetings once they learn the Eight Building Blocks. In chapter 8 each part of the format is explained in detail. At this time your purpose is to simply give the students an overview of what will happen at a class meeting.

Class Meeting Format

The format for class meetings is as follows.

1. Compliments and appreciations
2. Follow-up on prior solutions
3. Agenda items
   a. Share feelings while others listen
   b. Discuss without fixing
   c. Ask for problem-solving help
4. Future plans (field trips, parties, projects)

We recommend you teach the Eight Building Blocks while students are in the circle. You are beginning a new tradition and setting up a different way of relating to each other.

▼ Building Block 1: Form a Circle

Tell students that the first step in the class meeting is to create an atmosphere in which win-win solutions can take place and in which everyone has an equal right to speak and be heard. A circle arrangement—without any tables or desks—allows everyone to see everyone else, and it will remind students that the class meeting is a different and special part of their experience at school.

Some teachers prefer to tell their students exactly *what* they want and then ask for ideas about *how* to accomplish it. For example, they might say, "We are going to move all the desks against the walls and move our chairs into a circle. Who has some ideas about how to accomplish this quickly, quietly, and respectfully?"

The students then share their ideas about how to arrange the circle with the least amount of chaos. It is helpful to give elementary students the task of finding ways to form the circle quickly, quietly, and respectfully. Safety issues are usually discussed under "respectfully" or can be added as another consideration. Really listen to their ideas and review their proposals instead of telling them what to do. They love seeing their ideas written on the board. When they think they have a plan that will work, they're ready to move the furniture. If possible, find a student with a stopwatch to time the class (or use a clock). Let the kids get started without any additional instruction from you.

Other teachers simply tell the students to form a circle and then watch to see what happens. Classes often end up with many different arrangements. For example, one class we heard about formed a square with the tables, and students sat on top of the tables. Another class stacked all the tables in the corner and made a circle with the chairs. Another class pushed the tables and chairs to the back of the room and sat in a circle on the floor. Let the kids be creative. If their first try doesn't work, discuss it and let them come up with some new possibilities. This is a great opportunity for kids to learn that it is okay to make mistakes and learn from them by trying again with new information.

After all the furniture is moved, write on the board how long it took. Ask the kids if they have any ideas for improvement. Encourage them to discuss the process. Without realizing it the kids are having the first discussion that will set the tone for future meetings. They are learning by doing, not by being lectured; you are showing and allowing them to be involved. Ask them if they would like to put the room back to normal and try again to see if they can cut down on the time. Sit back and enjoy observing how much kids can learn from doing something, discussing it, and trying again.

Each person in the classroom needs a space in the circle. If anyone is left out, ask the students to scoot backward to make room. Some teachers prefer to make a seating chart, assigning seats in the circle. This decision is up to you. It is important, however, that all students, classroom aides, and the teacher are in the circle before continuing. If the class decides to sit in a circle on the floor, the teacher must be seated at the same level and in the circle with the students.

▼ Building Block 2: Practice Compliments and Appreciations

It's important to start the class meeting on a positive note, and it's a real boost to everyone's self-esteem when students and teachers say nice things to one another. Since most kids aren't used to giving compliments, we suggest using the first class meeting to teach them how. One way is asking them to think of a time when someone said something that made them feel good about themselves. They can take turns sharing their examples with the group.

Another suggestion is asking your students to think about something they would like to thank others for. Give examples. Perhaps they would like to thank a classmate for making a poster or lending a pencil. Maybe they would want to thank someone for playing catch or jacks with them. They might like to thank someone for walking to the playground with them or for being a friend by eating lunch with them. It doesn't take many examples before the kids get the idea and can think of something they appreciate.

Another way to teach compliments is to ask the kids to think of something they wish someone would compliment *them* on. Then ask the person seated on the student's left to give that compliment to the person who suggested it. For instance, Whitney might wish someone would compliment her on how hard she is trying not to talk out of turn. She tells this to the class. Zack, seated to her left, says to Whitney, "I would like to compliment you on how well you are doing not talking out of turn." Whitney should respond with, "Thank you." You would then ask Zack if he has something he would like to be complimented on and continue the procedure. Some teachers object that these compliments don't sound sincere. Keep in mind that the activities we have suggested are for practice. The awkwardness disappears and sincerity takes over as students learn the skill of giving and receiving compliments.

You can also teach compliments by asking your students, "What do grown-ups usually do when they get a compliment?" Emphasize that it's hard even for grown-ups to give and receive compliments, because compliments often don't focus on what someone does. If we focus on what someone does, others will get a better idea of what we like. For instance, a student might say, "I want to compliment you for letting us have class meetings," which is much more informed than simply saying, "You're a nice teacher."

Students can also learn to make their compliments and appreciations specific. If someone says "You're nice," you can help the student be more specific by suggesting that they say, "You're nice because _____," or ask the student to give an example of something the person did that he or she thought was nice.

If students are having a hard time coming up with compliments, remind them how easy it would be if they were asked to think of criticisms and put-downs instead. One teacher said to his class, "Isn't it a shame how easy it is for us to be negative and how hard it is for us to be positive? Wouldn't it be nicer if we had more positives in our lives? Let's keep practicing until this gets easier."

It helps to give students examples of statements that might seem like compliments at first but that aren't really very encouraging. These are called back-handed compliments. You can ask the students, "What's wrong with this compliment?" and then give an example, such as "I'm glad you like me better than you like the rest of the kids," or "I'd like to compliment you for sharing your candy with me, because usually you are very selfish."

If someone gives a compliment that is really a criticism, ask that person if he or she would like to try again or ask for help to turn the criticism into a compliment. If the person who gave a back-handed compliment can't think of a way to change the statement, ask for suggestions from the class. This models the helping rather than the hurting principle. It is also okay for students to pass, but it is important not to let a criticism slide by without addressing it.

A primary teacher helped her students learn about compliments by suggesting that students be careful not to say things that could hurt the hearts of others. The students had no difficulty with this concept and were able to share examples of how they felt when someone "hurt their heart."

Spend some time on how to receive a compliment. We recommend that people acknowledge compliments with a simple "thank you," so the person who gave the compliment knows it was heard.

Once students understand how to give a compliment, help them take turns by using an item—such as a bean bag or talking stick—that can be passed around. Send the item around the circle with these instructions: "When you're holding the item in your hand, you can either give a compliment, tell someone what you would like to be complimented on, or pass. In other words, you can say 'give,' 'get,' or 'pass.' Give means you have a compliment you would like to give to someone. Get means you would like to get one. Pass is obvious."

We have witnessed several classrooms that have implemented the idea of give, get, or pass. It is impressive to witness students who feel comfortable asking for what they need when they would like to "get" a compliment. Some teachers ask for a show of hands from anyone who would like to give a compliment to the person who has asked for one and then let that student choose someone to give her a compliment. Even more impressive is the response from so many students who raise their hands to show their willingness to give a compliment to anyone who asks—even students who were not treated well before class meetings are implemented.

Another activity is to ask students to volunteer to make posters, such as the one shown in figure 3.1. Posters can serve as a reminder and add a sense of fun.

At first the kids may feel uncomfortable or think giving compliments is silly. If you stick with the activities so they can practice, the skills will grow and so will the good feelings in the classroom. Many teachers who have class meetings regularly tell us that students complain when a meeting is called off because nothing is on the agenda. They say, "Well, we could at least do compliments."

Giving compliments may be embarrassing to junior high school students. They seem to find the words *appre-*

> **Two, four, six, eight.**
> **What do we appreciate?**
> **Compliments,**
> **Appreciations,**
> **Acknowledgments.**

Figure 3.1

ciation and *acknowledgment* easier to use than the word *compliment*. Ask questions to warm them up. For instance, you might ask the students to tell about something that really makes them angry, to talk about some activity they like to do, or to share their favorite food or music. Such topics are nonthreatening, and they give students an opportunity to break through barriers and get to know one another better.

▼ *Building Block 3: Create an Agenda*

Let your students know that you will set up a notebook for agenda items—any problems or issues with which teachers or students want help. Students and teachers can write their concerns on the agenda during the day. It may become disruptive when students congregate and linger around the agenda book. To avoid this kind of disturbance, have the kids determine specific agenda-setting times, such as just before leaving the room for recess or lunch.

In the beginning some teachers use a shoe box for agenda items. They may use green paper on Mondays, blue paper on Tuesdays, yellow paper on Wednesdays, etc., to help follow some chronological order in dealing with the problems. Using a shoe box helps alleviate the problem of retaliation when someone sees their name on the agenda. Let students know that it may take time for them to fully comprehend that the purpose of class meetings is to help people, not to hurt them, and that no one is in trouble if they're on the agenda. Eventually students will understand that it is a nice experience to have their name on the agenda because the whole class will join in the project of looking for beneficial solutions, and they can then choose the one they think will help them the most.

Some teachers ask students to put problems on the agenda without names so they can work on general solutions. This is fine in the beginning. However, accountability is increased when students learn that they won't get into trouble for problems and that every problem is an opportunity to learn and to help each other.

The only items that will be handled at the class meeting are those that are on the agenda before the meeting. Between meetings, remember to put items on the agenda instead of trying to solve problems yourself when they occur. If a student comes to you complaining about another person in the class, say, "That's something we can talk about at the class meeting, unless you see another solution that would work for you on our Wheel of Choice. [See chapter 7, page 110.] If you would like to bring up the item at our class meeting, would you please add it to the agenda?" This approach serves two functions. It saves time (you don't have to deal with every problem), and it gives the students real problems to solve at the class meeting.

Many teachers want to start problem solving right away. We strongly suggest you wait until you have taught all of the Eight Building Blocks before dealing with items on the agenda. Encourage your students to start putting concerns on the agenda so you will have things to work on as soon as they learn the skills.

Forming a circle, reviewing the meeting's purpose and format (including establishing the agenda), and learning about compliments are enough topics for the first meeting. At the end of this meeting, let your students know when the next meeting will be, tell them where the agenda will be kept, and have them return the furniture to the normal arrangement.[2]

---

2. All of the activities mentioned in this and the following chapters can be found in the *Positive Discipline in the Classroom* manual by Jane Nelsen and Lynn Lott. In this manual the activities are written in a format that includes the objective, materials required, and step-by-step instructions that are easy to follow. The manual is available from Empowering People Books, Tapes, and Videos, 1-800-456-7770.

▼

Chapter

4

Strengthening Communication Skills

All mistaken attempts to resolve a conflict in a democracy
are based on either too little respect for others or too little
self-respect.

Rudolf Dreikurs

Communication skills, such as being a good listener, taking turns, expressing oneself clearly, and respecting separate realities, may be introduced at the second class
meeting after forming the circle and delivering compliments. The most effective way to teach skills is through
activities that help students discover through their own
experience what works and what doesn't work.

Experiential Activities

The most effective way to introduce activities is to follow
these four steps.

1. Explain the activity.
2. Demonstrate the activity with a volunteer student.
3. Let the students try the activity.
4. Allow them to process their responses by expressing their thoughts and feelings.

Although these steps may not be appropriate for every activity, we have found there is less confusion if students first hear about it, then see it demonstrated, and then try the activity themselves.

It is important to allow students to process their responses to the activity by sharing their thoughts, their feelings, and what they are learning. The main points you would like to make are usually made by the students when they express themselves. It is okay to make points that may have been missed *after* the students share their experiences. This is what we mean every time we ask you to "process the activity."

You may facilitate the process by asking, "What were you deciding about yourself, about the other person, about what are you learning, or about what you are going to do?" The answers to these questions provide a wealth of information about the long-range effectiveness certain behaviors have on students. For example, some students may say that they are feeling hurt or angry and are deciding to either "get even" or withdraw in the future.

▼ Building Block 4: Develop Communication Skills

You may choose any or all of the following activities to teach listening skills. You may even want to create some of your own.

Activity: Have all the kids talk at the same time. After a signal for them to stop, ask how many of them felt heard. A lively discussion may result when you ask them to express what they were feeling, learning, or deciding.

Activity: Ask for a volunteer to share an interesting experience, such as his or her favorite vacation. Have all the other kids wave their hands in the air to indicate they want to speak. Ask them to stop and then process with the volunteer about his or her feelings. Ask how many of them would find this distracting while they are talking.

Activity: Have each student pick a partner. One student tells the other about a favorite TV show while the other refuses to make eye contact. Then have one partner actually get up and walk away while the other is talking. Process this activity by inviting the students to share their thoughts, feelings, and decisions based on their experience.

As students express what they are learning from these activities, you will find that everyone is getting the message about poor listening skills. Ask them to discuss how these activities relate to the success of class meetings. Whenever they aren't using good listening skills during class meetings, you can ask, "How many of you think we're practicing good listening skills? How many do not?" Kids can show their answers by raising their hands. Usually nothing more needs to be said in order for the problem to correct itself.

Taking Turns

Suggest to the kids that one way to avoid the problems generated by poor listening at a class meeting is to take turns going around the circle during a discussion. It is effective to use an object that can be passed from student to student, such as a bean bag, a toy microphone, or a talking stick. When a student has the object, he or she can make a comment, give a suggestion, or pass. It is empowering for quiet or shy students to have something tangible symbolizing personal power and the option to take a turn if they choose. Many teachers have observed that the only time some of their students share their thoughts and ideas is during a class meeting when they have the object in their hands.

In the beginning some students need more guidance than others. Guidance can be in the form of questions: "How many of you think it's important that we take turns so everyone is listened to with respect? How many of you would like a whole room of people who can help each other with problems? How many of you think we can find solutions to problems instead of using punishment and humiliation?" The fact that they are asked instead of told and that they have an opportunity to raise their hands to show agreement gives them a sense of inclusion and ownership.

"I" Statements

Part of good communication is to use "I" statements. Have the kids practice "I" statements by thinking of a time when they were very happy. Have them fill in the blanks to the following: "I felt happy because _____, and I wish _____." Then have them think of a time when they were angry and do the same.

Feelings can usually be expressed in one word. You may wish to ask the kids to develop a list of feelings such as happy, angry, embarrassed, afraid, sad, excited, and so on, and take the time to practice "I" statements and words that express feelings.

Once kids learn the skill of using "I" statements, they have a reference point when communication breaks down. For instance, if you think someone is communicating in a blaming or judgmental way, you might ask the student, "Would you be willing to try again using an 'I' statement, or would you like help from the class?" If the student wants help, let him or her choose a suggestion from someone whose hand is raised.

Solutions, Not Blame

Introduce the concept of focusing on solutions instead of blame. Guide a discussion about this important point: "If you are looking for blame, what will you find?" (Blame.) "Once you establish blame, then what?" (You can focus on blame forever and not make any changes.) "If you look for solutions, what will you find?" (Solutions.) "Which direction is the most productive, focusing on blame or on solutions?" (Obviously, solutions.) Ask for a volunteer to make a poster like that in figure 4.1 to hang in the room.

**We are
looking for
solutions—
not blame.**

Figure 4.1

Respect

Stress the importance of avoiding humiliation and judgment in order to create an atmosphere of respect. Give the kids a chance to talk about times when they felt hurt or criticized so that the class has some examples of disrespectful behavior. You might want to start the discussion by sharing some experiences of your own. At the end of the discussion, ask for volunteers to make two more posters (see figures 4.2 and 4.3).

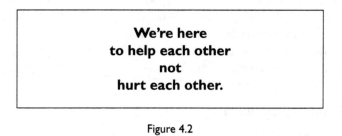

**We're here
to help each other
not
hurt each other.**

Figure 4.2

**Mutual respect
practiced
here.**

Figure 4.3

Win-Win Situations

Discuss the difference between a win-lose situation, in which someone has power over others, and a win-win situation, in which everyone experiences power. Students are used to adults who try to have power over them. When kids begin class meetings, they may think this is their time to have power over adults or over each other. Instead, let the kids know that for the class meeting to be a safe place, everyone must work together to find win-win ideas. A poster like figure 4.4 could be a good reminder.

We Decided

Some classes like to make a list of guidelines for creating respectful class meetings. Ask students to brainstorm sug-

**Give and Take
for
Win-Win Power**

Figure 4.4

gestions about what they need from each other to feel safe. Write all their ideas on the blackboard. Ask them to choose three to five suggestions they think are the most important. Ask for a volunteer to make a "We Decided" poster, and print the three to five suggestions on the poster. It might look like the one in figure 4.5.

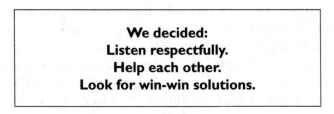

**We decided:
Listen respectfully.
Help each other.
Look for win-win solutions.**

Figure 4.5

Some teachers begin every class meeting by asking students to recite three or four basic guidelines. Mrs. Binns asks her first-grade students, "What are our basic class meeting rules?" She will then call on several students until they have remembered all four rules: (1) don't bring anything except yourself to the circle, (2) keep all six legs (your own two legs plus the four chair legs) on the floor, (3) only one person speaks at a time, and (4) we are here to help each other, not to hurt each other.

▼ Building Block 5: Learn About Separate Realities

It is impossible to understand human nature and behavior without understanding about separate realities.[1] Most adults claim that they understand that everyone is different, thinks differently, and has different perceptions and different goals. Yet when it comes to their own behavior in dealing with the behavior of children, they often act as though there is only one way, and it is "my" way. Teachers often act as though all children should hear them exactly the same way, understand and accept their goals and what they say in exactly the same way, and that they should then all behave in the same way—obediently. Children who don't fit this mold are often punished. This is very disrespectful, and children usually respond in their own disrespectful ways. This creates a cycle of disrespect.

Many adults are afraid that the only alternative to punishment is permissiveness. Permissiveness is very disrespectful for children, for adults, and for the order that is necessary for freedom. When we truly understand separate realities and act on this understanding, we will have many tools to help encourage children and to invite cooperation instead of rebellion or obedience.[2]

---

1. This topic is explored thoroughly in Jane Nelsen, *Understanding: Eliminating Stress and Finding Serenity in Life and Relationships*, rev. ed. (Rocklin, Calif.: Prima, 1996).
2. "To be successful in today's society, children need skills other than those based on obedience. In fact, obedience can be dangerous. Young children who have learned obedience are at high risk to follow the promptings of gang leaders and delinquent peers who may lead them into drug abuse or other hazardous activities. They are likely to find themselves equipped for very few jobs as they may lack the skills of cooperation: communication skills, problem-solving skills, self-discipline, personal accountability, and respect for self and others." Jane Nelsen, Roslyn Duffy, Linda Escobar, Kate Ortolano, and Debbie Owen-Sohocki, *Positive Discipline in the Classroom: A Teacher's A–Z Guide* (Rocklin, Calif.: Prima, 1996), 21.

An understanding of separate realities is an important building block in order for class meetings to help teachers and students break the cycle of disrespect. The following activity is a fun way to encourage people to understand and respect differences.

Tell your students you would like to play a game that helps people understand that not everyone is the same or thinks the same way. Ask, "How many of you sometimes think there is always a right or wrong answer? How many think there's only one way to see things? How many sometimes feel embarrassed to raise your hand because you think everyone knows the answer but you? We're going to experiment with an activity that will demonstrate that there are at least four different ways to look at things."

Activity: Collect pictures of a lion, an eagle, a turtle, and a chameleon. (Some teachers have stuffed animals or just write the animal names on a large piece of paper.) Ask the kids, "If you could be one of these animals for one day, which one would you like to be?"

Once the students have made their decisions, have them divide up into four groups, one for each animal. Ask someone from each group to list all the characteristics the group members like about their animal at the top of a large piece of paper. At the bottom, have them list the other animals and all the reasons they *didn't* choose to be that animal. Show them the following example of how their sheets can be organized.

Why We Want to Be the Lion

Why We Didn't Choose		
Eagle	**Turtle**	**Chameleon**

Below are some responses from several high school classes, in case you need to help the students with further hints or instructions.

Why We Want to Be the Lion		
king of the jungle	independent	strong
playful	respected	people respond
proud	sociable	to the roar
warm	good looking	passionate
takes care of		
personal needs		

Why We Didn't Choose		
Eagle	**Turtle**	**Chameleon**
bird of prey	plodding	changes to fit in
violent	vulnerable	insincere
endangered	avoiding	cold blooded
flighty	too slow	not centered

Why We Want to Be the Eagle

observe	protected	gentle
fly	beautiful	symbol of great
soar	faithful	country
freedom	aware	independent
strength	respected by	keen eyes
long living	Native Americans	masters
control of destiny	in charge	
great view	intelligent	

Why We Didn't Choose

Turtle	Chameleon	Lion
slow	too changeable	dangerous
hard shell	run from	hot, dry, arid
hide	problems	aggressive
weak	blend in too	lazy
bottom of	much	loud
totem pole		macho
not attractive		bad hair days

Why We Want to Be the Turtle

sturdy	long-living	relaxed
protected	cool environment	persistent
wise	enduring	independent
gentle	steady	calm
can hide from	predictable	symbolize earth
danger	reliable	lay in sun
look at details	peaceful	
patient	friendly	
don't hurt	don't bother	
anyone	anyone	
know how to	trusting	
enjoy selves		

Why We Didn't Choose		
Lion	**Eagle**	**Chameleon**
fierce	power hungry	moody
gruesome	loners	volatile
violent		phony
destructive		unreliable
arrogant "kings"		inconsistent
ruthless		not very strong
lazy		sneaky
predatory		unpredictable
loud		
cunning		
hunted		

Why We Want to Be the Chameleon		
changeable	passive	harmless
unusual	accommodating	understanding
adaptable	listener	flexible
observer	cute	sensitive

Why We Didn't Choose		
Lion	**Eagle**	**Turtle**
loud	superior	avoid
power hungry	unapproachable	bite
meat eater	unadaptable	slow
aggressive		defensive
lazy		

Hang the papers on a wall next to each other. Ask which group would like to go first. Then ask for a volunteer from that group to read all the reasons they wanted to be their animal. Then ask another person from that group to read all the reasons why other people didn't want to be their animal. Be prepared for laughter and comments from the groups, and remind them that they will have an opportunity to share their thoughts and ideas after every group has a turn. Ask each group to take turns reading why they wanted to be their animal and why others didn't.

After all the groups have had a turn, ask the students what they learned from this activity. Most of the following points will come from the students: people see things differently, what one person sees as a bad thing another person might see as a good thing, everyone has strengths and weaknesses. Continue the discussion by pointing out that any quality can be positive or negative and that there is no one right way to be.

Ask the students what the advantages might be if a classroom had some of the qualities of each of the animals represented. What might some of the disadvantages be? How could we all be better by contributing our strengths and learning from each other about how to overcome our weakness? What would happen if we all focused on the strengths of others instead of the weaknesses? How can this information be helpful at a class meeting?

Once your students have learned the communication skills and respect for separate realities outlined in this chapter, they will know how to create an atmosphere of respect that guarantees effective class meetings. In the next chapter we will show you how to give students a deeper knowledge of separate realities by discussing the Four Mistaken Goals of Behavior.

Chapter

5

Why People Do What They Do

Discouragement is at the root of all misbehavior.

Rudolf Dreikurs

The observer, by his unconscious choice, determines what he will see.

Rudolf Dreikurs

Children are always making subconscious decisions based on their perceptions (separate realities) of their experiences in life. They are making decisions about themselves: am I good or bad, capable or incapable, significant or insignificant? They are making decisions about others: are they encouraging or discouraging, helpful or hurtful, do they like me or dislike me? They are making decisions about the world: is it safe or scary, nurturing or threatening, a place where I can thrive or a place where I need to survive? Again, children are not aware that they are making these decisions that center on their need to belong and feel significant; however, the decisions they make become beliefs that affect their behavior. Based on their beliefs, they either thrive or survive.

When children feel safe—that they belong and are significant—they thrive. They learn, they develop into capable people, and they develop social interest. When children believe they do not belong and are not significant, they adopt survival (defensive) behavior. Survival behavior is often called misbehavior. Survival behavior is based on mistaken goals of how to find belonging and significance and may take the form of trying to get undue attention, negative power, or revenge, or by giving up. They are called mistaken goals because children who choose them do not attain their primary goals of belonging and significance.

The following chart provides a wealth of information about the Four Mistaken Goals of Behavior. Many teachers keep a copy of this chart on their desks as a quick reference to help them understand their own feelings and the feelings and beliefs of children when a problem occurs. The last column is especially useful for specific interventions that are encouraging and empowering.

Most "misbehavior" will fit into one of these Four Mistaken Goals of Behavior. Rudolf Dreikurs was once asked, "How can you keep putting children in these boxes?" Dreikurs replied, "I don't keep putting them there. I keep finding them there." An important building block for effective class meetings is to teach children about these mistaken goals so they can use encouragement to help each other. When children feel encouraged (belonging and significance), their need to misbehave will disappear. Understanding the Four Mistaken Goals of Behavior is another piece in the Positive Discipline puzzle. The more teachers realize that children's behavior is based on a

Mistaken Goal Chart

The child's goal is:	If the parent/ teacher feels:	And tends to react by:	And if the child's response is:	The belief behind the child's behavior is:	What the child needs and what adults can do to encourage:
Undue Attention (to keep others busy or to get special service)	Annoyed Irritated Worried Guilty	Reminding Coaxing Doing things for the child he/she could do for him/herself	Stops temporarily, but later resumes same or another disturbing behavior. Stops when given one-on-one attention	I count (belong) only when I'm being noticed or getting special service. I'm only important when I'm keeping you busy with me.	**Notice Me—Involve Me.** Redirect by involving child in a useful task. "I love you and ____." (Example: I care about you and will spend time with you later.) Avoid special service. Say it only once, then act. Plan special time. Set up routines. Take time for training. Use family/class meetings. Touch without words. Set up nonverbal signals.
Power (to be boss)	Angry Challenged Threatened Defeated	Fighting Giving in Thinking "You can't get away with it" or "I'll make you" Wanting to be right	Intensifies behavior Defiant compliance Feels he/she's won when parent/teachers are upset Passive power	I belong only when I'm boss or in control, or proving no one can boss me. "You can't make me."	**Let Me Help—Give Me Choices.** Acknowledge that you can't make him/her do something, and ask for his/her help. Offer a limited choice. Withdraw from conflict and calm down. Be firm and kind. Act, don't talk. Decide what you will do. Let routines be the boss. Get help from child to set reasonable and few limits. Practice follow-through. Redirect to positive power. Use family/class meetings.
Revenge (to get even)	Hurt Disappointed Disbelieving Disgusted	Retaliating Getting even Thinking "How could you do this to me?" Taking behavior personally	Retaliates Hurts others Damages property Gets even Escalates the same behavior or chooses another weapon	I don't think I belong, so I'll hurt others as I feel hurt. I can't be liked or loved.	**Help Me—I'm Hurting.** Deal with the hurt feelings: "Your behavior tells me you must feel hurt. Can we talk about that?" Use reflective listening. Don't take behavior personally. Share your feelings. Apologize. Avoid punishment and retaliation. Show you care. Encourage strengths. Use family/class meetings.
Assumed Inadequacy (to give up and be left alone)	Despair Hopeless Helpless Inadequate	Giving up Doing for Overhelping Showing a lack of faith	Retreats further Passive No improvement No response Avoids trying	I don't believe I can belong, so I'll convince others not to expect anything of me. I am helpless and unable; it's no use trying because I won't do it right.	**Don't Give Up On Me—Show Me a Small Step.** Take time for training. Take small steps. Make the task easier until the child experiences success. Show faith. Encourage any positive attempt, no matter how small. Don't give up. Enjoy the child. Build on his/her interests. Say, "I don't give up on you." Use family/class meetings.

mistaken idea instead of thinking of children as bad, the easier it is for teachers to be proactive and encouraging.

Understanding the
Four Mistaken Goals
of Behavior

Teaching Students About the Four Mistaken Goals of Behavior

After forming a circle, exchanging compliments, and choosing an agenda item, explain to the students that at this class meeting they will learn about the beliefs behind behavior. There is a belief behind every behavior. However, we usually focus on the behavior instead of understanding the belief. When the belief is changed, the behavior will change.

We are much more effective when we understand the belief that motivates a person's behavior instead of just dealing with the behavior itself. Perception modification is more effective than behavior modification for long-term effectiveness. Use this candle activity to demonstrate the power of dealing with the belief behind behavior.

Materials

1. Four candles of varying sizes to represent a mother, a father, a four-year-old girl, and a baby
2. Four small candle holders

3. Kitchen matches
4. The *Family Songs* audiotape[1]
5. A cassette tape player

Directions

1. Deliver the following short lecture: "There is a belief behind every behavior, but what do we usually deal with? The behavior. That makes as much sense as ignoring an arsonist who keeps setting fires. Dealing with the arsonist does not mean you don't also put out the fire. Dealing with the belief behind the behavior does not mean you don't deal with the behavior. You are most effective when you are aware of both possibilities, the behavior itself and the belief behind the behavior.

"Here's the classic example of a belief behind a behavior. Suppose you are a four-year-old girl. Mom goes to the hospital and brings home a brand new baby. What does the four-year-old see happening? Mom gives the baby lots of time and attention. What does the four-year-old interpret that to mean? Mom loves the baby more than me. What does the four-year-old do in an attempt to get the love back? She acts like a baby—whines, cries, wants a bottle, soils her pants. It is her belief that motivates her behavior."

2. Play a few lines of the song "Number One" on the *Family Songs* tape. Introduce it by saying, "I'd like to play a song for you that beautifully illustrates this point."

Oh, it's hard to be number one
And lately it's just no fun at all.
Life was so nice when we were three—
Mommy and Daddy and me.

---

1. Wayne Frieden and Marie Hartwell-Walker, *Family Songs*, audiotape (Orem, Utah: Empowering People Books, Tapes, and Videos, 1988); 1-800-456-7770.

When I was the only one,
Everyone noticed me.
They said what a cute little baby—
What a handsome child he'll be.
And now there's another,
And I don't like it one bit.
Send it back to the hospital and
Let's just forget about it.

3. Use candles for the following demonstration: "Now I would like to demonstrate what one mother did because she had a four-year-old daughter who was feeling displaced by the birth of a baby brother. One evening, when the baby was asleep, the mother sat down at the kitchen table with her daughter and said, 'Honey, I'd like to tell you a story about our family. These candles represent our family.' She picked up one long candle and said, 'This is the mommy candle. This one is for me.' She took a match and lit the candle as she said, 'This flame represents my love.' She picked up another long candle and said, 'This candle is the daddy candle.' She used the flame from the mommy candle to light the daddy candle and said, 'When I married your daddy, I gave him all my love, and I still have all my love left.' She put the daddy candle in a candle holder, picked up a smaller candle, and said, 'This candle is for you.' She lit a smaller candle with the flame from her candle and said, 'When you were born, I gave you all my love. And look. Daddy still has all my love, and I still have all my love left.' The mother put that candle in a candle holder next to the daddy candle, then picked up the smallest candle and, while lighting it with the mommy candle, said, 'This is a candle for your baby brother. When he was born, I gave him all my love. And look—you still have all my love. Daddy has all my love. And I still have all my love left because that is the way love is. You can give it all to everyone you love and still have all your love. Now look at all the light we have in our family with all this love.' "

4. Allow silence for the students to experience their feelings. Allow time for expressing feelings and thoughts. In addition to using the candle activity, leading a discussion is an excellent method of helping kids understand why people do what they do. Sometimes questions that require a simple "yes" or "no" answer are enough to get the class engaged and wanting to know more. At other times it is important to ask open-ended questions, the kind that inspire more than "yes," "no," and "I don't know" answers.

▼ *Building Block 6: Recognize the Four Reasons People Do What They Do*

Ask your students if they've ever wondered why people do what they do and if they would like to learn more. Usually they do, and they'll raise their hands to tell you their ideas. After hearing what they have to say, tell them, "In addition, there are Four Mistaken Goals of Behavior. To explain these four mistaken goals, I'd like to use the example of homework. What reasons do you think kids might have for not doing their homework?"

The kids will usually give such reasons as "I was too tired," "I had too much other work," "I lost it," "I didn't understand it," and so on. Explain that these are the rational excuses people give for their behavior. However, many times people do things for reasons that are not rational, and they may not even be aware of the reasons. We call these hidden reasons. The hidden reasons for behavior are based on our desire to belong and feel important. Ask, "How many of you want to feel like you belong and are important in your family, with your friends, and in the classroom?" Explain that all of us seek ways of belonging and being important. Sometimes they work, and sometimes they don't. If we think we aren't loved or don't belong, we usually try something to get the love back, or else we hurt others to get even when we think they don't love us. Sometimes we even feel like giving up because we think it's impossible to do things right and to belong. The things we do when we believe we don't belong and aren't important are often mistaken ways (or mistaken goals) of finding belonging and importance. They are called "mistaken" goals because they don't really help us achieve what we want. The Four Mistaken Goals of Behavior are listed below.

1. Undue Attention

2. Power

3. Revenge

4. Assumed Inadequacy (Giving Up)

Go back to the example of homework. Ask, "How many of you think some people might not do their homework because that's a good way to get the teacher or their parents to pay more attention to them? Have any of you ever decided not to do your homework to show your power and prove that teachers or parents can't make you do it—or at least they can't make you do it as fast as they want or as thoroughly as they want?" (Watch closely for nonverbal signals such as a grin, a flustered face, etc., which we call a recognition reflex.) Continue, "Maybe some of you have felt hurt and decided to get even by not doing your homework because you knew that would hurt your parents or teacher. Have any of you ever felt so discouraged that you believed you couldn't do your homework, so why try? Did you ever want to just give up and have people leave you alone?"

The Mistaken Goal Chart Activity

Ask your students to think of a time they felt unloved, thought they weren't special, or felt they didn't belong.

Mistaken Goal Chart			
Thinking/ Deciding	Feeling	Behavior	Mistaken Goal
	Irritated Worried Annoyed		
	Angry Mad Challenged		
	Hurt Upset Sad Disappointed		
	Hopeless Helpless		

Tell them to try to remember exactly what happened, how they felt, and what they decided to do. Give them about two minutes to relive the situation in their minds. Then put a chart with four columns on the board, like the one shown above. In the second column, list four groups of words that express feelings.

Ask your students to look at the chart and see if any of the feeling words apply to the situation they were thinking about. If they weren't able to think of a situation, all they need do is think of a time they had any of the feelings on the list. Ask for a volunteer to share his or her example. Find an example for each of the groups of feeling words. In the third column, write down what the volunteers did when they had those feelings. In the first column, write what the volunteers were thinking or deciding when they had those feelings. On the following page is a chart filled out by volunteers in a third-grade class.

Mistaken Goal Chart			
Thinking/ Deciding	**Feeling**	**Behavior**	**Mistaken Goal**
Teacher only pays attention to the smart kids	Irritated Worried Annoyed	I make funny noises and make fun of her when she's not looking.	Undue atten- tion (to keep others busy with me)
The play- ground supervisor tells me I have to eat lunch, or I can't play.	Angry Mad Challenged	I pretend to eat my sand- wich, but I hide it in my pocket	Power (to be boss)
Someone called me "Fatso."	Hurt Upset Sad Disappointed	I said, "You're ugly." I cried so no one could hear me.	Revenge (to get even)
I'll never be able to do my times tables!	Hopeless Helpless	I said, "I hate math and I think it's stupid." I threw my paper in the trash.	Give up and be left alone

After filling in the chart, explain to your students that everyone gets discouraged at times. When discouraged, we have those feelings, think those thoughts, or act those ways. In the chart, we can see that mistaken goals lead to misbehavior. For example, when a student feels she is not getting enough attention, she may seek undue attention by making funny noises when the teacher is not looking. Each mistaken goal leads to misbehavior as a mistaken attempt about how to find belonging and significance. This is why they are called mistaken goals. In the fourth column, write the mistaken goal—Undue Attention, Power, Revenge, or Assumed Inadequacy (Giving Up)— that corresponds to the behavior.

It is important to understand the different beliefs behind behavior in order to avoid using punishment as a solution. Once we understand the reasons why people do what they do, we might be able to think of ways to deal with their beliefs and to encourage them when they are feeling discouraged. The following activity will teach students how to use their brainstorming skills to encourage each other.

Encouragement

Activity: Have the students go back over each of the mistaken goals and think of things that would encourage a person who had those discouraging thoughts. Ask the kids what would make them feel better if, as in Undue Attention, they believed they are valued only if they are noticed or get special service. For Power, what if they believed they had to be the boss, do it their way, win, or show others they can't force them to do something? For Revenge, what would be encouraging for students who believe it's okay to hurt others or themselves because *they* feel hurt? For Assumed Inadequacy, what would motivate those who believe it's better not to try, who wish everyone would leave them alone because they are sure they aren't good enough or can't do things right?

As the class brainstorms encouragement ideas, write them down on a chart, such as the one shown on page 83, for future class meetings. To help the kids generate ideas, ask, "How could a person get attention or special treatment without misbehaving? How could a person have power in useful ways, to help others instead of to defeat others? How can people handle hurt feelings without hurting themselves and others? How can

81

people get help learning a skill or learn that it's okay to make mistakes?"

On the facing page is an encouragement chart filled out by a fifth-grade class.

After the class has completed this activity, you might want to present some practice situations so that they can guess the mistaken goal and suggest appropriate encouragement. Remind the students that all we really can do is guess and that it isn't up to us to tell others why they do what they do. If we guess correctly, we may help others become aware of their hidden reasons, which is often helpful. Even if we're wrong, that gives us information to build on.

When guessing is done with a friendly, helpful attitude, the people we are guessing about usually let us know if we're right because they feel understood. Sometimes they let us know by a smile of recognition, and sometimes with a simple "yes" or "no." The important point is that they know we're trying to help, not to hurt or stereotype.

Use the following examples to let students practice their new knowledge of encouragement. (Explain that these are imaginary names and situations.)

Example 1. Jesse refuses to turn in a homework assignment even though it is completed.

Example 2. Emily leaves her seat twenty times a day.

Example 3. Serita carves on her desk.

Example 4. Charlie always walks in two minutes late, and the whole class has to stop what it's doing to wait for him to sit down.

Example 5. Luke calls someone names on the school bus.

While any of the above behaviors could be based on more than one belief, damaging property or hurting another person is usually a form of revenge. When we have

Encouragement Chart			
Undue Attention	**Power**	**Revenge**	**Assumed Disability**
Walk with them to school.	Ask for their ideas.	Tell them you are sorry if you hurt their feelings.	Let them help someone else with something they are good at.
Sit by them at lunch.	Let them be a line leader.	Be their friend.	Tell them they are okay.
Laugh at their stories.	Put them in charge of a project or chore.	Invite them to your birthday party.	Have another student work with them.
Talk to them.	Ask for their help to tutor another student.	Compliment them.	Tell them math was hard for you, too.
Let them have a special job.	Ask them to teach the class how to play a game.	Ask them to play a game with you.	Let them do the things they are good at.
Ask them to play.	Tell them you feel angry when they boss everyone around.	Give them a hug.	Tell them they will get it when they are ready.

a real situation on the agenda and make guesses about the belief, one way we know we've guessed correctly is if the person misbehaving lets us know. Another way is to watch the person's body language and look for a recognition reflex. Remember that people are often unaware of the belief behind their own behavior, but when their motivation is guessed in a friendly way, they usually see the truth and feel understood. (They can also tell when people are trying to guess in order to have information to use against them.)

Activity: One class decided to make signs to put on the ends of popsicle sticks for each of the mistaken goals. Each student had a set of four. They agreed that if anyone was behaving in a disruptive way, they would guess what the mistaken belief might be and hold up their sign. The intent would not be to label, blame, or stereotype, but it could be seen by the disruptive person as a friendly reminder. The misbehaving student could then decide if he or she would like to choose contributing behavior instead of disruptive behavior.

There is an amusing footnote to this story. Guess who got the Power sign the most often? The teacher. This good-natured teacher would say, "Okay, okay. I can see that I'm trying to boss you around. Who has some ideas about what I could do to invite cooperation?" This teacher modeled that it is not "bad" to make a mistake and that the group can help each other make effective changes.

Activity: Play the *Behavior Songs*[2] for each of the four mistaken goals. After each song ask (with a sense of fun) if any of the behaviors mentioned in the songs sound familiar. You can also watch for recognition reflexes (laughter, grins, head nodding) while the songs are being played. Lead a discussion on what the kids think about the mistaken belief in each song and their suggestions about how the kids in the songs could be encouraged.

Even though these activities are time consuming, you are laying the groundwork for respectful and effective problem solving. Don't be too surprised if student behav-

---

2. Wayne Frieden and Marie Hartwell-Walker, *Behavior Songs*, audiotape (Orem, Utah: Empowering People Books, Tapes, and Videos, 1988); 1-800-456-7770.

ior starts improving spontaneously. We are all often unaware of why we do what we do. That's why it can be helpful just to hold up a mirror. Students will also have more understanding and compassion for other students, and the atmosphere in the classroom will improve.

In the next chapter, students will practice role playing and brainstorming as methods of solving problems. They will be much more effective and encouraging when they understand separate realities and the Four Mistaken Goals of Behavior.

Chapter 6

Effective Problem-Solving Skills

All opinions are correct from the point of view of the observer.
Rudolf Dreikurs

Many of the skills children need to be successful, happy, contributing members of society are learned through problem solving. Effective problem-solving skills help students understand their role of responsibility within the classroom or any system. Problem solving helps them think, speak, and interact thoughtfully with others. These skills will help students be more successful in all aspects of their lives.

▼ Building Block 7: Practice Role Playing and Brainstorming

By the third class meeting students are usually ready to learn effective problem-solving skills. Form the circle, exchange compliments, and then tell the class that today they will learn two new skills that will help them solve problems: role playing and brainstorming. Choose an item from the agenda that you think provides opportunities for practicing these skills. (Once students have learned class-meeting skills, you will discuss agenda items in chronological order.) Another option is to choose a typical problem, such as cutting in line or name calling. Sometimes it is less threatening to learn role playing when dealing with a problem that doesn't involve specific students. Remind them that today, learning the skills is more important than solving the problem.

Sometimes Discussion Is Enough

Sometimes role playing and brainstorming are not necessary for solving a problem. Do not underestimate the value of a simple discussion. By discussing an issue, kids get a chance to voice their opinions, share their feelings, and give suggestions. Because they are *actively involved* in a respectful discussion, students seem to hear each other better than they hear lectures from teachers or accusations from each other. Their comments or suggestions can be both amusing and irritating—often they say the same things you have said, which went in one ear and out the other. You can choose to feel frustrated and discounted or be grateful that the kids listen to each other and come to your conclusions—or to better ones.

Although a discussion can be enough to help kids become aware of the need to make changes, there are times when it is easier to succeed at problem solving by incorporating brainstorming and/or role playing.

Role Playing

Before setting up the role play, ask how many students have ever role-played before. Point out that role playing is like putting on a play where class members pretend to be different people involved in the problem they want to solve.

It's fun to play a guessing game with the students to see if they can guess the two secret guidelines for role playing. Say, "I have two secret guidelines for role playing in my mind. Who wants to guess what they are?" They'll make all kinds of guesses, such as you have to listen, you have to take turns, you have to do what the teacher says, you have to use a soft voice. Then you say, "Those are good ideas, and we should use all of these. However, the two secret guidelines I have in my mind are: (1) you have to exaggerate, and (2) you have to have fun."

Kids almost never guess there could be a "rule" that you have to have fun. In the guessing process, not only do the kids become engaged, but you get to learn more about what they think. With younger students, you may need to explain the meaning of exaggeration.

Since some students are victims of perfectionism in our society, you may need to give them permission not to worry about playing a part perfectly, explaining that everyone will learn more if the players exaggerate the behaviors as a way of speeding up the demonstration of life experiences. Remind them that the role play is an opportunity to learn and to help each other—it is not a test of perfection.

Have the student who put the issue on the agenda describe a recent occurrence of the problem. Tell him or her to describe the episode in enough detail so that the class will know how to role-play the different parts. If the story doesn't include enough detail, ask some of the following questions: "What happened? Then what happened? What did you do? What did the other person do? What did you say? What did the other person say?"

If you have chosen a typical problem that does not involve specific students (yet), ask for volunteers who will describe what it might entail. After the problem has been described, ask the class to think of themselves as movie directors. Their first assignment is to think about the issue and figure out how many players are needed to act it out. List all the parts on the board. It is usually effective for the person with the problem to play the person with whom they are having the problem. This gives the student a chance to experience another point of view. But there are many exceptions to this guideline. The people involved in the problem may benefit most by watching the role play. Boys can play girls' parts and vice versa.

Based on the problem description, review the spoken lines and actions of each player, and ask for volunteers to play out the scene. Have them act out the scene in the middle of the circle, and remind them not to worry whether it's right or not. A role play need not last longer than one or two minutes. It doesn't take long for role players to identify with the parts and generate feelings and information. If, after playing it out once, any changes are needed to make it more accurate, they can try again. Kids love to role-play and sometimes beg to replay the scene over and over. They especially like playing the part of the teacher and watching the teacher pretend to be one of the students.

After the role play, ask the players what they were thinking, feeling, learning, or deciding according to the parts they were playing. It's very important to have the students express their responses after each role play so they can learn the results of what is happening. For example, a punishment may stop the behavior and seem to solve the problem. But the student may decide, "I'm a bad person" or "I'll get even later." When asked what they are learning in the role they are playing, students may realize that they are learning blame and fault finding instead of understanding and problem solving. Processing responses can help students find solutions to problems that will lead to healthy, long-term results.

One girl was upset with a boy who threw food at her in the cafeteria, so she put this on the agenda. The students loved role-playing this scene. When asked what they were thinking, feeling, or deciding, those who were role-playing others in the cafeteria said it was fun and scary. Some were afraid they might get in trouble, and they wished an adult would do something. The boy playing the food thrower said it was fun and that he felt good because everyone noticed him. The girl playing the target of the food throwing felt upset and embarrassed and didn't want to go back to the cafeteria again. Understanding feelings and decisions gives students valuable information that they can use when it is time for brainstorming.

Brainstorming

After the role play teach your students about brainstorming—a process in which they think of as many ideas as possible in a short period of time. When brainstorming, it's fun to think of silly or outrageous ideas to start the creative juices flowing. Silly ideas often lead to practical ideas. Every opinion is important, so write every idea on the board. During the brainstorming time, don't analyze or criticize any suggestion. Writing a brainstorm suggestion down doesn't mean it could really work; it's just a suggestion. Explain that there will be time later to eliminate suggestions that might be impractical or disrespectful.

Recording every suggestion tells all students that every opinion is important and worthy of consideration. When students know they can present an idea without being judged, it frees them to take more chances to contribute instead of playing it safe for fear of looking foolish. Once the list of suggestions is completed, discuss each one and let the students conclude what ideas would or would not be effective solutions. Then let them decide what ideas can be crossed off the list because of disrespectfulness or impracticality.

For students who use brainstorming time to be silly, writing down their ideas often influences them to stop shouting out things they don't really mean. One day during a brainstorming session, one of the students suggested "yell at them." The teacher ignored the suggestion. The student started repeating her suggestion in a louder and louder voice until the class meeting was disrupted. If the teacher had written down the suggestion right away, the student might have stopped.

In another classroom, a student suggested tying a student to his desk. The teacher wrote it down without saying a word and went on to the next suggestion. The student who gave the disrespectful suggestion looked a little deflated because his comment didn't create the negative attention he usually received. Rudolf Dreikurs called this "taking the sail out of their wind." Many people think that what we really mean to say is "taking the wind out of their sail," but think about it this way: students blow wind (misbehave) to try to activate your sail (get you to react). Taking the sail out of their wind means that you don't react. Misbehavior often stops when students don't get the usual reaction.

When the brainstorming was finished, the other students decided to eliminate that suggestion from the list because it wasn't respectful. Once students have learned respectful brainstorming, it may not be necessary to eliminate disrespectful suggestions from the list because they aren't chosen anyway when students are asked to choose the suggestion that will be the most helpful.

Brainstorming can be used with or without role playing; however, role playing should usually be followed by brainstorming. After the role play tell the kids it's time to brainstorm. Explain that anyone can give a suggestion of what would make the situation better. Remind them that there are no right or wrong answers during brainstorming. Sometimes ideas that seem impractical or even impossible give rise to good solutions. Sometimes silly suggestions help people lighten up and start being creative. Here is the list the students generated by brainstorming after role-playing the food-throwing problem.

1. The boy who threw food could apologize.
2. The girl could throw food back.
3. A teacher could tell them to stop.
4. The boy could be sent to the office.
5. The girl could move to another seat.
6. The girl could tell the cafeteria monitor.
7. The girl could say, "Stop throwing food at me."
8. The girl could ignore it.
9. The girl could wear a catcher's mitt.

A volunteer was asked to read aloud all the suggestions. The student who put the problem on the agenda was asked to choose the one she liked best from the list of ideas. She chose number four, sending the boy to the office. The teacher asked her how that would help her: "Would it make you feel good if he gets in trouble?"

The girl thought about that and then asked if she could change her mind. She chose number one, having the boy apologize. The teacher asked the boy if he would be willing to apologize now at the class meeting or later in private. He agreed to apologize now, which he did. The boy was then asked which of the suggestions would help him the most. He said that the apology helped because he hadn't meant to upset the girl. This example illustrates four important class-meeting techniques.

1. Have the suggestions read aloud. (Some teachers ask one student to read aloud all the suggestions. Others let the whole class read them together.)

2. Allow the student who put the problem on the agenda to choose the suggestion that will be most helpful. If another student was involved in the problem, invite that student also to choose a suggestion that would be helpful.

3. Ask, "How will that help?"

4. Allow the student(s) to choose one of two times for following through on the chosen suggestion.

When students are allowed to choose the suggestion they think will be most helpful, they are increasing their accountability and responsibility. Students are encouraged to think of long-range results when asked, "How will that help you, the class, or another person?" Choosing when they want to follow through on the suggestion increases their sense of power in a useful direction. Whichever solution is chosen, it should be tried for at least one week. If it doesn't work, anyone can put the issue back on the agenda.

If the students involved in the problem can't agree on a solution, invite them to think about it and let the class know the next day what they think would help solve the problem. Suggest to them that they could also let the class know if the discussion has been enough to solve the problem.

Some teachers voice their concern that this method is letting kids "get away" with misbehavior; we encourage them to "trust the process." What usually happens is that the behavior stops. (And isn't that more important than making the kids pay for past indiscretions?) There are several reasons to explain why the behavior stops.

1. A respectful discussion may be enough.
2. The students don't get the "usual" payoff. Believe it or not, punishment is a small price to pay for getting undue attention, winning the power struggle, or getting revenge.
3. The student feels a sense of belonging and significance after being treated respectfully by the teacher and peers. This is often enough to change the belief that motivates the misbehavior in the first place.
4. Positive peer pressure takes place when other students are trying to create an atmosphere of respect.

Voting

Voting is appropriate when the problem being discussed involves the whole class, such as which kind of party they would like to choose from the brainstorming list or which plan they like best for handling recess problems, line problems, cafeteria problems, etc. In some cases a majority vote is appropriate, but there are some cases in which it is imperative for the class to reach consensus.

A consensus is needed if a majority vote on a solution would leave a disgruntled minority to use their power to defeat or get revenge on the rest of the class. Since one of the goals of class meetings is to teach students to find solutions that everyone can live with, it is better to wait for consensus than to expect students to agree to a solution that won't work for them. Most problems presented for solving are not the kind that pit one part of the class against another.

Sometimes students are content to go along with a majority vote as long as they know the suggestion will be tried for a week and then re-evaluated. If it isn't working, they can brainstorm for more possibilities.

Appreciations

A helpful and positive conclusion to the problem-solving process is encouraging students to express appreciations. After the class has role-played, brainstormed, and chosen a suggestion to try for one week, ask the students if anyone has an appreciation for the person who put the problem on the agenda, for the role players, or for the person who made the mistake. Encourage students to be honest and to speak directly to the person, using positive statements to let them know their contribution is appreciated.

For example, in a class where the item on the agenda was about a boy who insulted another student, one girl who had experienced similar insults said during the appreciations session, "I want to thank you for bringing this up. A lot of kids make fun of me, and I never knew what to do. Now I have an idea of how to handle it next time it happens to me." Another student said, "I want to thank you for bringing this up because it was so much fun to role-play. I like to tease people, and the role play gave me an acceptable way to do it."

Dealing with Problems Outside the Classroom

There are two ways to deal with problems occurring outside class. One is to help the person with the problem decide what he or she can do, since it is impossible to control other people. The other way is to invite the other person or people to the class meeting and involve them in the problem-solving process.

It came to Mr. Ryan's attention that some of his students were misbehaving on the school bus. He asked them to pretend they were the bus driver. Then they went around the circle and expressed what they thought it would feel like to be the bus driver and what frustrations and problems they would experience. They went on to talk about some of the problems the bus driver was complaining about on the bus. He didn't want them to play games because he had to wait too long for them to put things away and get off the bus. This was messing up his schedule because he had to make double runs.

The solution the students came up with was to be allowed to have games on the bus as long as they used them appropriately and put them in their knapsacks before the bus reached the school. They also proposed that if the games were used inappropriately, the bus driver or teacher could confiscate them but would give them a chance to try again in a week.

The kids picked a committee of two to meet with the bus driver in question, tell him they had discussed the problem at their class meeting, inform him of their suggested solution, and ask if he would be willing to try it out. He said, "Yes."

A week later the bus driver appeared at the class meeting to thank the students for their cooperation. He said he'd had this problem for years, and this was the first time anything worked to solve it.

Use your judgment about the maturity of the kids and your own comfort level for handling complaints about other teachers. For example, one teacher felt comfortable allowing her students to discuss the problems they were having with another teacher because the kids had learned to be respectful. The students' solutions all focused on what they could do to avoid problems. They even decided that the teacher needed encouragement and made suggestions about how to do that.

The Power of Class Meetings in Difficult Situations

When kids get really skilled at problem solving, they can be extremely encouraging. In one school, a class had a problem with a student who came to school smelling badly of urine. He was a bed wetter. The kids teased him mercilessly on the playground. Someone put the problem on the agenda, and the students gave suggestions that would be helpful rather than hurtful. They learned that the boy didn't have a washing machine or even a shower at home. One of the students offered to have him come by his house every morning to shower and put on clean clothes, which he could wash the night before in their washer.

In one school where every teacher was using class meetings, the special-education teacher described in a faculty meeting how bad she felt when the other kids called her students such names as "retards." All the teachers agreed to discuss this problem in their class meetings. They asked the students several questions, such as how they felt when people teased them and called them names. They asked if they had ever thought about how much it must hurt the special-education students when they called them names. Most kids really don't think about the long-range results of their behavior unless they are invited to do so. They were asked, "How many of you feel good about being mean to others?" None of them admitted this possibility. The students in each class were then asked for suggestions to solve the problem of hurting other people through name calling. They came up with solutions that went beyond eliminating the name calling by deciding on ways to help the special-education students feel included in their games and activities.

In still another school, a little girl was killed in a car accident. The crisis team decided to use class meetings to help the kids deal with their grief and their fears. In each class they replaced compliments with a celebration of how this little girl had touched them. Each student had a chance to express an appreciation for the girl who had died. Then the teachers asked their students, "What are your concerns now?" Some of them were afraid to go home. Many had never dealt with death before and didn't know what to do. They brainstormed and found several suggestions. One was to set up a phone tree so they could call each other, even in the middle of the night. They came up with a list of people they could talk to during the day. Many kids had different people they felt they could talk to during school hours: janitors, librarians, a lunchroom supervisor, counselors, teachers, the principal, and each other. It was decided that students could get passes to go talk to someone whenever they felt the need. They decided to make pictures of the girl on a ribbon pin, which they wore for a week in her memory. They planted a tree, which they purchased and nurtured throughout the year in memory of the girl. The kids became role models for adult school members on the many ways to deal with grief.

Bronia Grunwald, coauthor with Rudolf Dreikurs and Floy Pepper of *Maintaining Sanity in the Classroom,* is a teacher who used class meetings for more than twenty-five years. Bronia had such faith in the class-meeting process that she asked to teach all the problem kids. Her philosophy was, the more problems, the more opportunity to teach problem-solving skills. She also had classrooms with more than forty students. During an interview she said, "That many students made more work correcting papers and having conferences with parents, but I also had more students to help solve the problems." Even though Bronia had mostly problem students, by midyear their behavior problems were eliminated because they had learned mutual respect, cooperation, and problem-solving skills.

But Bronia did not simply coast through the rest of the year. When she'd notice that a colleague was having trouble with a student, during a class meeting she would ask her students, "How would you feel about inviting Janey from Mrs. Smith's class to join our class? She is having problems. How many of you think we could help her?" Every time, her class would enthusiastically agree to invite a problem student into their class so they could use their skills to help.

We hope you're developing an understanding of how class meetings can empower students. Where else do they have their thoughts and ideas taken seriously? Where else do they have an opportunity to learn life skills that build confidence, courage, and self-esteem? Where else do they have an opportunity to nurture each other and learn respectful interactions? How could these benefits not create a classroom environment that enhances academic learning as well as emotional growth? Everything improves in a nurturing climate. Students and teachers can flourish.

▼

Chapter
7

Focusing on Solutions Instead of Punishment

There are no ills created by democracy that can't be cured by more democracy.

Rudolf Dreikurs

Any form of punishment or permissiveness is both disrespectful and discouraging. Punishment is based on several false premises:

1. In order to make children "do" better, first we have to make them "feel" worse.

2. It is more important to make children "pay" for what they have done than to "learn" from what they have done.

101

3. Children learn better through control and intimidation than through exploring the results of their choices in a nurturing environment.

Common forms of punishment found in our schools include the following: sending students to the principal, having students pick up garbage on the grounds (even though they didn't put the garbage there), calling home to tell parents their children are in trouble at school, putting children's names on the board, humiliating students in front of their classmates, giving students punitive time outs, and giving them detentions and suspensions.

Most teachers mean well when they administer punishment. They believe punishment is the best way to motivate students to behave properly. If the misbehavior stops for a while because of punishment, they may be fooled into thinking they were right. However, when teachers become aware of the long-range effects of punishment on students, they naturally want to learn more respectful methods of motivating students to behave properly.

The long-range results of punishment are rebellion or compliance. Compliance may seem like a good thing, but not when the price is low self-esteem, reduced confidence, and blind obedience. Some students who are punished comply. However, their behavior is often motivated by the fear of getting into trouble instead of the desire to cooperate out of respect for self and others. Other students openly or passively rebel in response to punishment. In any case, punishment creates the development of an external locus of control instead of an internal locus of control based on self-discipline and social interest.

When you first begin to hold class meetings, you may notice that students tend to think up very punitive suggestions while brainstorming. Many of their ideas are modeled on their experiences with punitive parents and teachers. Children live what they learn. Punishment has no place in the Positive Discipline classroom.

Teachers must take the first step to eliminate humiliation and punishment in order to create an environment that is nurturing, respectful, and conducive to learning. Teachers can help young people follow their lead by teaching skills for finding solutions that are nonpunitive. You will need an entire class meeting (after compliments and follow-up on prior solutions) to teach the eighth and final building block for effective class meetings. Explain that the meeting will be dedicated to learning another important form of encouragement, using nonpunitive methods for dealing with problems. The focus will be on finding solutions instead of using punishment.

▼ Building Block 8: Focus on Nonpunitive Solutions

Start with an activity that helps your students increase their understanding of the negative effects of punishment. Use one or both of the following activities.

Activity 1: Ask the following questions and write the students' answers on the board: "What is the first thing you want to do when someone hurts you? What do you want to do when someone bosses you? What do you want to do when someone calls you names or puts you down? How many of you think any of these things help you behave better? What would help you behave better?"

Don't be surprised if some students do think that punishment motivates them to do better. This may be due to several possibilities: (1) They may believe this because they have heard it from adults for so long, but their behavior doesn't match their belief. In other words, even though they believe punishment motivates them to do better, they don't do better after being punished.

Dreikurs used to say, "Watch the movement." Pay more attention to the tongue in the shoes (what people do) than to the tongue in the mouth (what people say). (2) It may be true that a fear of punishment motivates them to do better, but only when they think they might get caught. In other words, they have developed an external locus of control. (3) A fear of punishment motivates improved behavior, but the price is low self-esteem and a fear of taking risks. These students become "approval junkies" and depend on the opinion of others for their sense of self-worth.

Study the list of ideas students mentioned when discussing what would help them behave better. Ask them to discuss which of these would fit under the heading of encouragement and which would fit under the heading of discouragement.

Ask for a volunteer to make the following poster to help the class remember that encouragement is more effective than punishment.

**Where did we ever get the crazy idea
that to make people
do better,
first we have to make them
feel worse?
People *do* better
when they *feel* better.**

Activity 2: Ask the students to think of a time when someone tried to motivate them to do better by making them feel worse. If the students don't mention grounding,

My Punishment	What I Decided About Myself and/or Others	What I Decided to Do
Stay after class.	The teacher is stupid.	Stay after, pretend to work.
Call my parents.	I'm in trouble. I need to figure out how to get out of it.	Tell my parents the teacher lied.
Write sentences.	This is boring and stupid. I'd better not get caught again.	Write the sentences and then do what I want.
Name on board.	I don't care.	Experience the punishment, but don't change.

spanking, scolding, and taking away privileges, make sure you add them to the list. Ask them to try to remember exactly what happened as though they were reliving the event and to recall how they felt. As a result of that experience, what did they decide about themselves, about others, or about what to do? Invite sharing, one student at a time. Make a chart like the one above, and list the answers as well as all the things that were done by way of punishment.

Ask the students, "How many of you think that the students in the above example are deciding to be more responsible and cooperative in the future? What other things do you think they might be deciding to do in the future?"

Although children hate being punished themselves, they can be very reluctant to give up the power to punish others. It takes time for them to learn to use power in positive ways instead of trying to have power over others. Teachers have to learn positive ways before they can be taught and modeled for students. The first step is to go beyond consequences.

Going Beyond Consequences

In the first edition of this book, we encouraged the use of logical consequences. For several reasons we are now discouraging that concept and encouraging people to focus on solutions.

1. Too many teachers and students misuse the concept of logical consequences. They try to disguise punishment by calling it a logical consequence.

2. Rudolf Dreikurs taught that logical consequences are appropriate only for the goal of Undue Attention, yet most adults and students try to use consequences for all behaviors. Dreikurs also said that logical consequences are only one possibility for dealing with Undue Attention.

3. Misused consequences often make class meetings look and feel more like a kangaroo court than a nurturing place where students can help each other explore the consequences of their choices and learn from their mistakes.[1]

An amazing difference in brainstorming takes place when students focus on solutions instead of consequences, as the following example illustrates. During a class meeting, students in a fifth-grade class were asked to brainstorm logical consequences for two students who didn't

---

1. For those of you who feel comfortable using logical consequences and know how to keep them respectful, related, and reasonable, see the appendix for information on how to teach your class about them.

hear the recess bell and were late for class. Following is their list of consequences:

1. Make them write their names on the board.
2. Make them stay after school the same number of minutes they were late.
3. Take away from tomorrow's recess the same number of minutes they were late today.
4. Take away all of tomorrow's recess.
5. Yell at them.

The students were then asked to forget about consequences and brainstorm for solutions that would help the students be on time. Following is their list of solutions:

1. Everyone could yell together, "Bell!"
2. They could play closer to the bell.
3. They could watch others to see when they are going in.
4. Adjust the bell so it is louder.
5. They could choose a buddy to remind them that it is time to come in.
6. Someone could tap them on the shoulder when the bell rings.

The difference between these two lists is profound. The first looks and sounds like punishment. It focuses on the past and making children "pay" for their mistake. The second list looks and sounds like solutions that focus on "helping" the students to do better in the future. The focus is on seeing problems as opportunities for learning. In other words, the first list is designed to hurt, the second is designed to help.

The second step in teaching students to use power is teaching them the Four Rs of Solutions in positive ways.

Teaching the Four Rs of Solutions

Continue with Building Block 8 by teaching the Four Rs of Solutions. Inform the class that their job is to find solutions to solve a problem in the future instead of looking for ways to make a person pay for past mistakes.

Activity: Have the class work on a problem about an imaginary student who wrote on her desk. On the board list the following five suggestions for solving that problem:

1. Have the girl sit on the floor for a week.
2. Have the girl clean all the desks in the room.
3. Make the girl clean her desk while everyone watches.
4. Have the girl apologize.
5. Ask the girl if she would like to clean her desk now or before she leaves for the day.

Now tell the students about the Four Rs of Solutions: Related, Respectful, Reasonable, and Revealed. Related means the solution is directly related to the behavior. For example, when students don't do their homework, sending them to the office is not related to missed homework. A related solution would be for them to make up the homework or not get points for that assignment. Respectful means that teachers and students maintain a respectful attitude in their manner and tone of voice. It also means following up on the solutions with dignity and respect: "Would you like to make up the homework assignment during lunch recess or right after school?" Reasonable means you don't add punishment such as, "Now you'll have to do twice as much." Revealed means the students know in advance that if they don't do their homework, they'll need to make it up or else risk getting a poor grade. To make this point with your students, ask, "How many of you would feel it would be respectful if you had to experience a solution for something you didn't know about? For instance, suppose the teacher decided that anyone who sat in a certain chair would be suspended, but she didn't tell anyone?"

Go over the list of the five suggestions on the board. For each suggestion, ask, by a show of hands, "How many think this suggestion is related, respectful, and reasonable? We'll assume that all the solutions were revealed in advance." Cross out the suggestions that do not fit the criteria of the Four Rs of Solutions. Point out that when a solution meets all four Rs, it will probably be a good alternative to punishment.

Many teachers have switched from logical consequences to the Four Rs of Solutions. Once students have brainstormed for solutions to a problem, it is extremely important to let the individual student choose the solution he or she thinks will be most helpful. This encourages a safe environment for accountability to blossom.

Sometimes it is important to simply trust the process and let the students make mistakes. If a solution is not hurtful or humiliating, you might let it go and allow the students to discover why something that isn't related, respectful, and reasonable doesn't work. At the next class meeting, you can always put the new problem created by the mistake on the agenda. It is important to work on progress, not perfection. For example, one class decided that students who rocked their chairs back onto two legs should have to stand behind their chairs for the rest of the class meeting. The whole class agreed that this would be a helpful solution. However, the problem was soon put back on the agenda. They decided it was too disruptive to have some people standing. They also decided to see if the discussion was enough to solve the problem. It must have been, because students stopped rocking their chairs back after that.

Helping Students by Using the Wheel of Choice

A teacher in Bakersfield, California, created a Wheel of Choice as a shortcut to help her students use respectful, nonpunitive solutions. We have expanded the wheel by adding choices that provide solutions that meet all four Rs. Going over the wheel with the class and posting it for all to see meets the fourth R, Revealed.

Wheel of Choice
Try at least two of these ideas
when you have a problem.

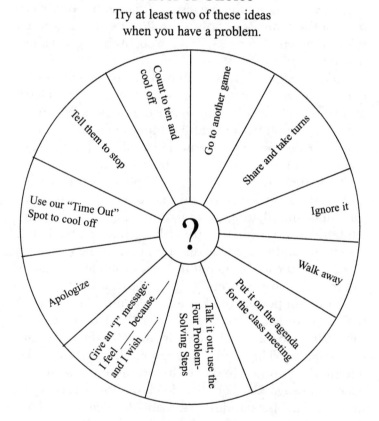

After you have tried at least two solutions—
or in an emergency—
GET AN ADULT TO HELP.

Activity: Show the students the Wheel of Choice and ask if they can either demonstrate or explain what each solution would involve. Even though the students may have learned about some of these options in earlier class meetings, it is important to take time for training and review the options at this time. If your students have forgotten how to give an "I" message, you can refresh their memory with this example.

Write down the formula the class learned in Building Block 4: "I feel _____ because _____, and I wish _____." Now ask if they could think of a way to fill in the blanks if someone started pushing in line. If the class is having difficulty, you can prompt them using the following, "I feel *worried when you push in line* because *I might get hurt,* and I wish *you would wait quietly until we can all leave together.*"

Ask the students if they can think of other problem-solving ideas that could be added to the wheel. Have the students check to make sure each suggestion meets the Four Rs of Solutions before adding it to the Wheel of Choice.

Trust the Process

Giving up the use of punitive solutions requires a mental shift. Kay Rogers, a recently retired teacher from Sharon School in North Carolina, said, "After I heard about the possibility of focusing on solutions instead of consequences, it was the hardest habit for me to break. All my life I had believed that kids learned from punishment—or at least from consequences. I can now see that my students and I both tried to disguise punishment by calling it consequences—even though the consequences weren't as harsh as blatant punishment. I had to learn about the effectiveness of focusing on solutions right along with my students. We were all surprised by the difference it made

111

in our classroom. The level of respect and caring for each other was raised tenfold. Students became pleased to find their name on the agenda because they knew that they would have a whole room full of consultants to give them valuable suggestions. And the solutions they found were much more effective in changing behavior than anything we had done before."

When punishment is eliminated and solutions are both kind and firm, children gain self-worth that results from being respectful to themselves and others. When students experience these alternatives to punishment, they gain courage, confidence, and life skills that will help them live successfully in our society.

▼

Chapter

8

Putting It All
Together

Security comes from a feeling of being able to deal effectively
with anything life may have to offer.

Rudolf Dreikurs

In your preparatory class meetings, you have introduced,
demonstrated, and practiced the Eight Building Blocks
listed in chapter 3. Let's review them here.

Eight Building Blocks for Effective
Class Meetings: A Review

1. Form a circle.
2. Practice compliments and appreciation.
3. Create an agenda.

4. Develop communication skills.

5. Learn about separate realities.

6. Recognize the four reasons people do what they do.

7. Practice role playing and brainstorming.

8. Focus on nonpunitive solutions.

If you or your students don't understand any of the Eight Building Blocks, now is the time to review. Once you have the basics down, you can begin holding regular meetings that follow the class-meeting format reviewed below.

Class Meeting Format

The format for class meetings is as follows.

1. Compliments and appreciations

2. Follow-up on prior solutions

3. Agenda items
   a. Share feelings while others listen
   b. Discuss without fixing
   c. Ask for problem-solving help

4. Future plans (field trips, parties, projects)

Follow Up on Prior Solutions

The first thing to do after compliments is to check the status of what the students have learned at previous meetings. Follow up on the solutions chosen during problem-solving sessions. Remember that any suggested solution is to be tried for only one week, so it's important to ask if the solution has been working. If it hasn't, the student may wish to put the issue back on the agenda for future problem solving.

Agenda Items

When an agenda item is read, ask the student with the issue if he or she still wants help with it. Often the student will state that the problem has been solved. You may want to leave it at that or ask the student if he or she would like to share how it was solved. The fact that so many problems are solved before their turn on the agenda is an effective part of the class-meeting process. Sometimes they are solved because there has been a sufficient cooling-off period to eliminate the problem. Sometimes simple awareness (just having it on the agenda) works to solve a problem. Many times a problem gets solved because students use their problem-solving skills outside of the class meeting.

If the student still wants help, ask what a satisfactory solution could be. Ask the other student involved in the problem if he or she agrees. If not, ask that student what his or her idea of a solution would be. If both students agree, ask if they would try the solution for one week, and then move on to the next agenda item. Not all problems require role playing, brainstorming, or even class discussion. But if the students don't agree on a solution, have the rest of the class brainstorm for suggestions.

When students name other students on the agenda, many teachers prefer that they use the Four Problem-Solving Steps (discussed in chapter 11) before the problem is discussed in a class meeting. Their feeling is that it is disrespectful for students to bring up a problem involving other students if it hasn't first been discussed with others. This is a valid point. However, when students know that the purpose of class meetings is to help each other, it is also valid to seek the help of the whole class so they can enjoy the many ideas generated by brainstorming. When every problem is seen as an opportunity for learning, everyone can benefit every time a problem is discussed.

Many teachers have found that it works equally well to solve problems by substituting the words *a student* or *a person* for a specific name; that is, instead of deciding what to do about Bill pushing in line, the class can problem solve what to do if "a student" pushes in line. We encourage teachers to use whichever method feels most respectful and helpful to them and to their students.

Many teachers go around the circle twice when brainstorming so everyone has a second chance either to make a comment or to pass. This draws out the quieter students and gives the less courageous kids time to think and listen for ideas from their classmates. Brainstorming generates more ideas. Students who were first in the circle may think of other ideas as part of the brainstorming process.

Jeremiah, a student, made a comment about a problem. As the talking stick made its way around the circle, several students disagreed with him and gave their reasons. The stick was passed around the circle a second time. When it came to Jeremiah, he said, "I don't agree with myself." It is important to remember that the class-meeting process encourages thinking skills.

Sometimes as you go around the circle, there will be students who hesitate (they neither comment nor pass). Rather than passing them by and assuming they have nothing to say, ask, "Are you thinking or are you passing?" If they say they are thinking, ask, "Would you like us to wait while you think, or would you like us to come back to you?" When you present limited choices, students learn how to contribute usefully and can save face if the delay was merely a way of being silly or rebellious.

Another option for handling agenda items is to give students the choice simply to express their feelings. It's important to let kids know that it's okay to share their feelings, that feelings are always okay, and that feelings are different from actions. When a student is expressing feelings, it's important to listen without trying to fix the problem.

It's up to the person who put the item on the agenda to specify which approach he or she prefers.

If a student wants to talk about a problem that involves someone else—such as a bus driver, another teacher, a student who is absent, or the principal—remind the student that it is best to invite that person to attend the class meeting. If the person isn't willing to come to the room, the problem can be discussed only in terms of what the student can do.

Effective problem solving empowers students and encourages them to have confidence in their ability to help one another. It emphasizes that learning is a continuous process that includes mistakes and stresses the importance of respect for self and others. Dealing with the students' real concerns is a great advantage because it teaches them that they can come up with enough good ideas to help each other. They don't need to pass the buck by sending classmates to the principal for punishment. Teachers and students learn to see every problem as an opportunity for learning.

Future Plans

Take time during class meetings to plan a fun classroom activity, a field trip, a party, or a special treat. This time can be used creatively. One third-grade class discussed what to do when they got fidgety. The teacher had a tape player in the room. He agreed with his students that when they got fidgety, he'd turn on loud rock music and let them dance wildly for two minutes. When the music went off, everyone sat back down.

Once you have established regular class meetings, students will begin to feel closer to you and to each other. Setting up a party or time to play is a treat that everyone enjoys.

A sixth-grade class planned for a special game board tournament on Friday afternoons for students who had completed their assignments. Two weeks later they discussed solutions to help everyone complete their assignments so everyone could participate. (This problem was put on the agenda by a student.) They set up a system of class tutors for those who needed extra help. The teacher expressed her delight that she no longer felt the need to lecture and cajole (which didn't work anyway) because the students took over the responsibility of helping each other.

Special events should not be used as a punishment or a reward; they should be opportunities for learning. Part of the learning is to find ways to include everyone and to help everyone be successful, as in the following example from the book *Positive Discipline: A Teacher's A–Z Guide.*[1]

A south Texas high school had four teachers who worked as an academic team with students who had many at-risk factors, including poor performance in class, poor attendance, drug problems, undeveloped social skills, and inadequate self-control and self-discipline. A number of these students were in gangs.

The four teachers had been using permission to go on field trips as a reward for good behavior, but they soon noticed that the same students were going on every field trip. Being allowed to go didn't appear to be an effective incentive for good or improved behavior. Then the teachers were introduced to the concepts of Positive Discipline in the Classroom. They decided to use class-meeting time to involve all 180 of their students in planning the next field trip. The students were told that they would all get to go as long as they brought their signed permission slips from home.

1. Jane Nelsen, Roslyn Duffy, Linda Escobar, Kate Ortolano, and Debbie Owen-Sohocki, *Positive Discipline: A Teacher's A–Z Guide* (Rocklin, Calif.: Prima, 1996), 347–48.

The students planned the entire field trip during their class meetings. A few parent volunteers were also involved in the planning. On the day of the field trip, the teachers were nervous about how the students would behave, particularly those who had been excluded in the past because of their misbehavior. To the teachers' amazement all the students cooperated and contributed in positive ways to the experience. Even the lunch the students had planned to take place at a local park went off without a hitch. The manager of the place they visited told the teachers that he had never seen a group of high school students behave so well before. He said he planned to write a complimentary letter to the school's principal. When the students and the teachers evaluated the field trip during their next class meeting, everyone gave it high marks. Many students went on to say that the time they had spent connecting with each other in a positive fashion made them want to do more as a team.

The teachers noted that tempers didn't flare up as easily among the students after this field trip. They believed that this change occurred because the students had worked together to plan a successful event and had been given an opportunity to see one another in a different light.

Remember That the Process Takes Time

When young people are learning a new way of looking at things and new ways of handling problems, sometimes things get worse before they get better. If the students aren't responding with the enthusiasm you'd hoped for, don't be discouraged. Keep plugging away in small steps, and trust that they will all come together eventually to help the class. We have found that success is directly related to the teacher's commitment. When teachers believe that the life skills learned from class meetings are equally as important as academic skills, class meetings will be successful.

If you find your students struggling because of their lack of skills, use the class meetings to continue building skills before tackling items on the agenda. Remind yourself and your students that it's okay to take time for training. Even if the class meetings are difficult at first, don't give up. They will get better with practice. If you practice taking small steps, you'll see steady improvement. In our workshops, we say over and over, "Trust the process."

Some classes respond immediately; others take longer. We met with two teachers two months after a teacher in-service. They said, "We are so thankful that you warned us that it sometimes takes a month or more before things run smoothly. Our first class meetings were so discouraging that had we not received prior warning, we would have given up. We're glad we stuck it out because it has made such a difference in our classrooms."

In the next chapter we cover many skills that can enhance class meetings and Positive Discipline in the classroom.

Chapter

9

Expanding
Class-Meeting Skills

We learn from our mistakes only if we are not afraid to make mistakes.

Rudolf Dreikurs

Once you have become familiar with the basics of holding class meetings, you will soon notice how helpful it would be to have additional skills for dealing with difficult situations. As your skills increase you can help your students improve their ability to cooperate and succeed in class meetings. The skills in this chapter have been used successfully with students at all grade levels.

"How Is That a Problem for You?"

Sometimes it's enough to ask students the following question when their problem comes up on the agenda: "How is that a problem for you?" When they answer, it often becomes obvious to them what they could do to improve the situation without using brainstorming time to help them figure it out. This approach is especially useful with children who do a lot of tattling.

Eight-year-old Joey was bothered by two girls whispering next to him, so he put the issue on the agenda. The teacher asked, "How is this a problem for you?" Joey replied, "I can't get my work done because they're too noisy." The teacher asked Joey if he had any ideas about what he could do to improve the situation. He thought for a minute and said, "I could move and do my work somewhere else, or I could ask them to stop talking." The teacher asked, "Do you still want help with this problem from the class?" "I think I've worked it out," said Joey.

When going through the items on the agenda, asking, "Is this still a problem for you?" may eliminate taking class-meeting time to work on issues that have already been resolved. The question can also help students recognize that some things do not really concern them.

Mrs. Ritter had a student who put two other names on the agenda because the children were going into each other's desks and taking things. Mrs. Ritter asked, "How does this affect you?" The student said, "It doesn't." These two children had agreed that they could use each other's pencils and erasers, and it really didn't affect the student who put it on the agenda. They had worked out something that was fine.

Another child did a cartwheel in the hall. A student was able to say, "I put it on the agenda because it was not safe. He might get hurt or someone might get kicked."

This student was able to recognize how this might be a problem to him and to others.

Talking Versus Fixing

Some issues are too emotional or too complex to be solved at one class meeting. If you think the class may be ganging up on someone or if the class is blaming instead of searching for solutions, it might be helpful to tell the group that this is one of those issues where "talk time" is needed instead of "fix time." If talking doesn't help, the issue can be put back on the agenda for more discussion at the next meeting or until it feels appropriate to work on a solution. A cooling-off period may be needed before the issue can be discussed respectfully.

Trying again after a cooling-off period is only an option when the problem is one that is appropriate for the class to solve. If you know that you'll never agree with the students or that they are trying to change something in the school policy that is nonnegotiable, be honest with them. Let them know they can brainstorm about how to cope with the situation instead of trying to change it.

Mistakes As Opportunities for Learning

Sometimes students don't put items on the agenda. This may be because they feel others will think less of them if they can't solve problems alone. They might also believe they are supposed to be "perfect" and that putting an issue on the agenda would be a statement that they are "imperfect." If you think this may be the case, it's time to teach your students about mistakes.

We often ask teachers what they were taught about mistakes during their childhood. Ask your students a similar question. See if their answers are like the ones we get:

Mistakes are bad.

You shouldn't make mistakes.

You are stupid, bad, inadequate, or a failure if you make mistakes.

If you make a mistake, don't let people find out. If they do, make up an excuse even if it isn't true.

The next step is to help them explore decisions people make based on those messages. Ask how many of them have decided any of the following:

I'm bad when I make mistakes.

People will think less of me if I make a mistake.

If I make a mistake, I should try not to get caught.

It is better to make excuses and blame others than to accept responsibility.

If I get caught or accept responsibility, I will experience blame, shame, or pain.

I better not take risks if I know I can't do something "right" or perfect.

Explain that these are "crazy notions" about mistakes because they not only damage self-esteem, but they also invite depression and discouragement. It is difficult to learn and grow when we feel discouraged. Remind your students that we all know people who have made mistakes and then dug themselves into a hole trying to cover them up. We also know that people can be forgiving when others admit their mistakes, apologize, and try to solve the problems they have created.

Teachers have an opportunity to help students change misguided notions about mistakes. Many of your students play video games or computer games, so it may be helpful to talk about mistakes against this backdrop. When children make a mistake on a video game, they simply try again. It may take one hundred tries to figure out how to solve a problem or get to the next level. The computer or video game doesn't scold or shame the person; the games are set up to keep the player trying and to encourage the player to learn from past errors. Point out that life isn't all that different. Every person in the world will continue to make mistakes as long as he or she lives. Because this is true, it is healthier to see mistakes as opportunities to learn instead of statements of inadequacy. Teach kids that when the whole class really understands that we learn by making mistakes, individual students will not mind having their names put on the agenda. Instead they'll see it as an opportunity to get valuable help from their classmates. They'll actually learn to be proud to take responsibility for what they've done, even if it was a mistake, because they know it doesn't mean they are bad or will get in trouble. It means they are willing to be accountable—a necessary step to using mistakes as an opportunity to learn.

Hiding mistakes keeps us isolated; we can't fix mistakes that are hidden, nor can we learn from them. Trying to prevent mistakes keeps us rigid and fearful. Good judgment comes from experience, and experience comes from poor judgment. Ask for a volunteer to make the poster in figure 9.1 to encourage this new way of thinking about mistakes.

**Mistakes are
wonderful opportunities
to learn.**

Figure 9.1

125

Sometimes mistakes require us to make amends where possible, or at least to apologize. When students learn about the Three Rs of Recovery, they have a tool to use that takes the guilt, shame, and blame out of mistakes.[1]

The Three Rs of Recovery

Inform your students that making mistakes isn't as important as what we do about them. Anyone can make mistakes, but it takes a secure person to say "I'm sorry." If a student would like to make amends for a mistake, the Three Rs of Recovery can help him or her do so. Write these steps on the board for your students:

1. Recognize the mistake with a feeling of responsibility instead of blame.
2. Reconcile by apologizing to the people you have offended or hurt.
3. Resolve the problem, when possible, by working together on a solution.

Ask the students if they can think of a time when they made a mistake and could have used the Three Rs. You may wish to tell the following story about how a group of seventh-grade boys dealt with a mistake they made.

Mary was a student who had few friends and spent a lot of time in the counselor's office instead of with her classmates. One day she put an item on the agenda concerning a poor grade she had received. One of the boys blurted out, "Why don't you try studying for a change?" Two other boys laughed, and Mary appeared hurt by their comments. She turned her chair around and, although she didn't leave the room, she refused to continue the

---

1. For more information about the Three Rs of Recovery, see Jane Nelsen and Lynn Lott, *Positive Discipline for Teenagers* (Rocklin, Calif.: Prima, 1994).

discussion. The teacher said, "I can see Mary is feeling hurt. Boys, are you willing to use the Three Rs of Recovery? You may not have meant to hurt her feelings, but sometimes that happens whether you intend it or not."

All three boys said in unison, "Sorry, Mary. We weren't trying to hurt your feelings. We really do wish you'd pay more attention to your work so you could do better in class." Mary inched her chair a little closer to the circle but kept her back to the class. "Mary," said the boy who made the comment, "we made a mistake and we're sorry. We hope you won't stay angry with us." Mary left her chair in place but murmured, "It's okay."

The teacher then asked, "How many of you hate it when your feelings are hurt?" Half the class raised hands. "And what makes you feel better when that happens?" Some of the answers were, "I like it when the person apologizes," "I like it if someone walks with me so we can talk about it," and "I like it if someone gives me a hug."

The teacher suggested that after the class meeting, some of the students might do some of those things for Mary. After class, several students went up to talk to Mary and give her a hug. A meeting like this might change how students treat one another while helping students like Mary learn behaviors that invite friendship.

Encouragement Instead of Praise and Rewards

Rudolf Dreikurs, an Adlerian psychologist and author of *Children: The Challenge*, said, "Children need encouragement like a plant needs water."[2] Encouragement is a process of showing the kind of love that conveys to kids that they are good enough the way they are.

---

2. Rudolf Dreikurs, *Children: The Challenge* (New York: E. P. Dutton, 1987), 36.

Encouragement tells kids that what they do is separate from who they are, and it lets them know they are valued for their uniqueness without judgment. Through encouragement we can teach that mistakes are simply opportunities to learn and grow instead of something to be ashamed of. Children who feel encouraged also gain self-love and a sense of belonging.

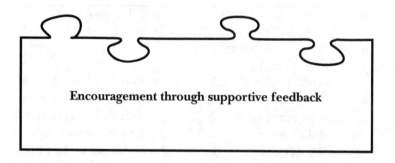

Encouragement through supportive feedback

Encouragement is the foundation for every concept discussed in this book. Encouragement through supportive feedback focuses on the language of encouragement.

If your students are having trouble coming up with nonpunitive and encouraging solutions to problems on the agenda, it may be time to teach them the difference between praise and encouragement. It's easy to praise or reward students who are behaving well, but what can we say to those who are misbehaving and not feeling good about themselves? These are the ones who need encouragement the most.

Use the following example to demonstrate the need for encouragement. What would your students say to a student who got As and Bs on his report card? They might respond, "You're doing so well. You must feel very good about that. You're really smart." What would they say if that same student earned only Ds and Fs? He still needs

Differences Between Praise and Encouragement[3]		
	Praise	**Encouragement**
Dictionary Definition	1. To express a favorable *judgment* of 2. To glorify, especially by attribution of *perfection* 3. An expression of *approval*	1. To inspire with courage 2. To spur on: *stimulate*
Recognizes	Only complete, perfect product	Effort and improvement
Attitude	Patronizing, manipulative	Respectful, appreciative
"I" message	Judgmental: "I like the way you are sitting."	Self-disclosing: "I appreciate your cooperation."
Used most often with	Children: "You're such a good little girl."	Adults: "Thanks for helping."
Examples	"I'm proud of you for getting an *A* in math." (robs person of ownership of own achievement)	"That A reflects your hard work." (recognizes ownership and responsibility for achievement)
Invites	People to change for others	People to change for themselves
Locus of control	External: "What do you think?"	Internal: "What do I think?"
Teaches	What to think	How to think
Goal	Conformity: "You did it right."	Understanding: "What do you think/feel/learn?"
Effect on self-esteem	Feel worthwhile only when others approve	Feel worthwhile without the approval of others
Long-range effect	Dependence on others	Self-confidence, self-reliance

---

3. This chart is based on a chart by parent educators and parenting class leaders Bonnie G. Smith and Judy Dixon, Sacramento, Calif.

supportive feedback, but it's a lot harder to think of positive things to say.

Ask the class if they would like to learn how to use encouragement instead of praise and to see how encouragement works even when a person is failing. Point out that praise and rewards teach kids to depend on the external judgments of others instead of trusting their internal wisdom and self-evaluation. A steady diet of praise and rewards inspires them to believe, "I'm okay only if others say I'm okay." It also teaches them to avoid mistakes instead of learning from their mistakes. Put up the Differences Between Praise and Encouragement chart to show more about the differences between praise and encouragement.

After looking at the chart together, go back to the example of the student who is getting Ds and Fs and see if the class can think of things they could say or do that would be encouraging. Following are some examples.

"How do you feel about your grades?"

"What happened? Do you have any idea why your grades are dropping?"

"Would you like some help improving your grades? I'd be happy to help you with your spelling words."

"Hey, anyone can have a bad report card. We still like you a lot."

"I bet you're feeling scared to show this to your parents. Can I walk home with you when you bring them your report card?"

Following are two fun class-meeting activities that encourage discouraged students. Pick a student who needs encouragement. Have him or her sit in the center of the circle and let students go around the circle taking turns saying an encouraging statement to the student, or ask the kids if they would like to practice giving encouragement by writing notes of encouragement to each other. They could pick a different student for each day, so that each student eventually gets notes of encouragement.

The class may also choose to have the teacher assign partners for the week. Each pair watches for encouraging things to say and do for each other. It is also each student's responsibility to have a compliment ready for the partner once or twice a week during the class meeting.

Encouragement goes a long way toward establishing a positive classroom and class-meeting atmosphere. The students will catch the spirit and will probably come up with other ways to practice encouragement in the classroom. Encourage them to do so!

Routines

Routines establish a sense of order and stability. Life is easier for everyone when there is a smooth rhythm to events in the day. A routine is something students can learn to count on; the routine itself becomes the "boss," so teachers or students do not dictate what will happen. It is more empowering for students to hear, "Who can tell me what is next on our routine chart?" than to hear, "I need you to do your spelling now." The first statement implies that the teacher is asking the students to check the routine and see what needs to be done, while the second suggests that the teacher should be controlling. Many students feel rebellious when told what to do, but they'll gladly do what needs to be done.

Setting up routines works especially well for scheduling class job times, deciding how materials will be distributed and collected, establishing the way students enter and leave a room or line up for recess in elementary school, and following procedures outside the classroom (such as assemblies, field trips, and the library). The class meeting is the perfect place to set up routines with your students.

Six Guidelines for Setting Up Routines

You can create routines that are predictable, consistent, and respectful to all by following the Six Guidelines for Setting Up Routines. Use these guidelines while working with your students during class meetings.

1. Focus on one issue at a time.

2. Discuss the issue when everyone is calm rather than during a time of conflict.

3. Involve students in developing a routine. Ask for their ideas. If they can't think of any ideas, use limited choices. For instance, ask your students whether they prefer to do math first or English first, or whether they'd like to have their art period before lunch or at the end of the day. (We talk more about limited choices in chapter 11.)

4. Use visuals, such as charts and lists. After the students agree on the order that things will be done, the teacher or one of the students can make a chart itemizing the routines. When it's time for reading, you can ask your students, "What is next on our schedule?" The schedule becomes the boss instead of the teacher.

5. Rehearse through role playing. Have the class pretend that it's time for the chosen activity, and go through a dry run so that everyone knows what's expected.

6. Follow through in a firm and kind manner. Once a routine is established, follow it faithfully. If a student questions or ignores a previously made agreement, ask, "What was our agreement?" Allow the student to experience natural or logical consequences but not punishment. For example, a student who doesn't turn in assignments receives a poor grade. A student who doesn't play respect-

fully on the playground loses that privilege until ready to play respectfully. Resist rescuing and lecturing. Rescuing is coaxing them to do their homework. Lecturing is anything other than stating the facts with dignity and respect. Help them explore what happened and what they can do about it: "What is our guideline for the privilege of playing on the playground? What are you doing? What will you need to do to have the privilege again?"

Establishing routines yields long-range benefits of security, a calmer atmosphere, and trust. Routines also help students develop life skills. They learn to be responsible for their own behavior, to feel capable, and to cooperate in the classroom.

Remember to be realistic and to understand that routines may not work perfectly at first. Students who are used to behaving in certain ways need time before they'll believe that their teachers mean what they say. Remind your students that it's part of human nature to resist change even when we know it's good for us. It is important to continue to follow the planned routine until students' resistance disappears.

Student involvement is the key to success with all of these class-meeting skills. The notion that teachers are isolated in a classroom can end when teachers use the class meeting and other positive-discipline methods as a way to utilize the valuable resources that surround them—capable young people. Student involvement is the secret to cooperation, collaboration, and healthy self-esteem for everyone in the classroom.

▼

Chapter

10

Questions and Answers About Class Meetings

Making mistakes is unavoidable, and the mistake is less important in most cases than what the individual does after he has made the mistake.

Rudolf Dreikurs

As you experience class meetings, many questions will arise. Here are answers to some of the most frequently asked questions from hundreds of teachers. Some questions are from elementary school teachers and some from junior high and high school teachers. Even though there are some developmental differences between students of different ages, there are many similarities. Teachers of all grade levels will find creative ideas for solving problems in the answers to all the questions. Watch for the basic principles of respect and empowerment in the answers. Hearing enough solutions based on dignity and respect will stimulate more creativity for empowering students—and yourself.

Questions Frequently Asked by Elementary School Teachers

Question: How do I avoid having students humiliated at a class meeting?

It is important to guide students away from any suggestions that would humiliate or hurt another student. Several questions help: "How would that be helpful for this person?" "How would you feel if that suggestion were given to you?" "Is that humiliating or respectful?" "Does that punish for past behavior or encourage change for future behavior?" "Is the solution related, respectful, and reasonable?" You might wait until all the suggestions have been made and then go over the list and ask the students which ones should be eliminated because they are not respectful, helpful, or practical.

Humiliation and punishment can be avoided by having the student with the problem choose the solution that would be the most helpful. Sometimes students do choose punitive solutions for themselves. To help them get out of the punitive mentality, you might ask, "How will that help and encourage you?"

Another way to avoid humiliation is through generalizing. This means talking about the issue in general terms instead of a specific problem involving a specific child. Suppose, for example, someone uses the agenda to accuse another person of stealing. This issue might be generalized by brainstorming for solutions. Ask the class, "What can we do to deal with the problem of stealing in general instead of looking for blame and trying to control one person?"

Another way to handle a situation in which you perceive that humiliation is taking place is to ask redirection questions: "How many of you would feel helped if you were in Johnny's place right now? How many of you would not?" "How many of you would feel ganged up on? How many would not?"

Generalization and redirection will be needed less often when kids catch on to the spirit of helping rather than hurting and punishing one another.

Question: Don't students get resentful when they ask for help and you tell them to put it on the class meeting agenda instead of helping them right away?

Actually, most students feel immediate relief just by putting their problem on the agenda. Many do feel resentful because they are used to getting special attention from the teacher. Others are used to being taken care of instead of being involved in the helping process. Change (even for the good) is not always easy. Some may feel resentful at first but not after they experience the positive attention and help they can receive during class meetings, which is usually much more creative than the help they receive from teachers.

A second-grade student complained to her teacher, Mrs. Binns, that some boys were kicking her seat on the bus. Mrs. Binns suggested she put that problem on the agenda and ask the kids for help. The first suggestion was profoundly simple: "Sit behind them." A creatively complicated suggestion was, "Get on the bus and put your books in one seat, then sit in another seat. When the boys sit behind you, you can move to the seat where your books are." There were many other suggestions, but the student chose the suggestion to watch where the boys sat and sit far away from them. (See chapter 11 for other suggestions that deal with requests for help.)

Question: How many times should students be allowed to put something on the agenda in one day?

Put this question on the agenda and ask the kids. One teacher had been allowing two or three items per person each day, and the issues were endless. He put the question on the agenda, and the students decided on the rule of one item per person each day. There hasn't been a problem since they discussed the issue and made the decision.

Question: What do you do if the kids won't pick a suggestion?

One possibility is to ask the whole class if they think it would be okay to see if the class-meeting discussion might be enough to motivate change. If not, the problem can be put back on the agenda and they can try again.

Another possibility is to ask the reluctant chooser if he would be willing to think about it, find his own solution, and report back to the class tomorrow. If he still seems reluctant, ask if he would like to choose two classmates to brainstorm with him during a recess period. It is rare for students to be reluctant to choose a suggestion that is truly helpful—once they make the shift in their thinking that class meetings are not punitive. Teachers need to display persistent faith in their students' abilities to find solutions when they are taught the skills and are given the opportunity.

Questions Frequently Asked by Junior High and High School Teachers

Question: Is it okay to move students who sit next to their friends and create a lot of disturbance at the class meeting?

This problem comes up frequently. Mr. Burke noticed his students had a difficult time being respectful when they were sitting next to their friends. He tried lecturing them about being inconsiderate. When that didn't work, he decided to separate the sets of friends. The kids responded with hostility and resistance to the whole idea of class meetings.

Mr. Burke decided to put the problem on the agenda. He asked his students the following questions during a class meeting and got the following responses.

1. What problems do you think we might have when friends sit together? The students brainstormed the likely problems, such as talking, giggling, and passing notes.

2. What suggestions do you have for solving these problems? The students agreed to be respectful so they could have the privilege of sitting with friends.

3. What would be a related, respectful, and reasonable solution if people don't keep their agreements to be respectful while sitting with a friend? The students decided that being separated from their friends for the rest of that meeting would solve the problem.

Predictably, nothing was effective until the students became involved in the problem-solving process. Although they often come to the same conclusions that teachers try to impose on them, the results are totally different.

Question: Are sixth-graders too immature for class meetings? The kids in my class act silly, make fun of each other, and sometimes are jerks to each other.

Developmentally, sixth-graders are beginning to respond more to peer influence than to adult influence. They also want to fit in with their classmates, so if negative behavior gets started, it may be difficult to stop.

Students sometimes act silly because teachers start holding class meetings before they teach the skills. One teacher who was having difficulties told her students that she had made a mistake by starting class meetings without teaching more skills. After two months of not doing much more than forming a circle, teaching basic skills, and exchanging compliments, the students settled down and were ready to use problem-solving skills.

Question: If the students are uncomfortable or embarrassed exchanging compliments, would it be okay to skip that part of the meeting?

We think that the compliment process is extremely important and that it is best not to let it be an option. Students (and adults) overcome the embarrassment stage of *giving and receiving* compliments when you stick with it. Still, as long as the opening activity is positive and results in the students learning more about each other so that they can begin to give compliments, variations are possible.

One possibility is to use this time to get to know each other by asking a question about outside interests, special hobbies, or other personal information. One teacher has a special book with thoughts for the day. She passes it around the class meeting and lets each student respond personally to the inspirational message.

A high school teacher teaching advanced physics with a group of students who had the reputation of being "nerds" and "brains" said, "If compliments are all you do, class meetings are worth it. Take as long as you need. The kids in my class get so much negative criticism that the compliments part of the class meeting was the first time some of them heard anything positive about themselves at school."

Question: Any ideas for handling backhanded compliments?

A simple way to handle a backhanded compliment is to say, "Oops, is that a compliment or an agenda item?" Another question that helps redirect a backhanded compliment is, "Would you please rephrase that until it sounds like something you would like to hear?"

Question: I am a resource teacher and have small groups of children for short periods at a time. I don't have time for class meetings.

There are two things you could try when problems arise in your classes. One possibility is to ask for a volunteer to put the problem on the homeroom agenda and let you know the suggestions brainstormed to solved the problem. Another possibility is to conduct a five-minute class meeting when a problem arises. When students and teachers are well trained in the class-meeting process, short meetings can be held in special classes where regular meetings are not held. However, short meetings do not work when teachers and students are not familiar with the process.

Question: Sometimes junior high and high school students feel like they're "ratting" when they bring up problems about other kids. How do I address this problem?

It helps to talk about how the class meeting is an alternative to suspensions and other unhelpful, punitive approaches. Remind students that it's normal to feel reluctant to "rat" on someone in a system that focuses on blame and punishment instead of accountability and solutions. Ask, "How many of you would want your name on the agenda if you knew people would gang up on you and try to get you?" Then ask, "How many would want your name on the agenda if you knew you would be getting thousands of dollars worth of valuable consultation from your peers that would be encouraging and empowering?"

Question: I've noticed a lot of complaints from students about other teachers at our school who are unwilling to hold class meetings. How do I handle this without making the other teachers look bad?

If kids have issues with teachers who won't hold meetings or discuss issues respectfully with them, it's important to help the kids focus on what they can do to take responsibility to solve their own problems. Remind them that we can't change others, just ourselves. If other teachers are willing, they could attend your meeting as guests to help work on a problem.

It helps to train all the faculty about class meetings and their potential. Remind them that human growth is about learning, and learning isn't smooth. The ultimate goal is to talk things over respectfully and solve problems. The fringe benefit is that there are fewer discipline problems, and positive motivation improves in classes that have regular class meetings. The more preparation the staff has ahead of time, the better they do with class meetings.

Question: Do I really need an agenda?

Yes. The agenda serves as a powerful, symbolic message that all students have the opportunity to voice their concerns while giving and receiving encouragement and practical help. The agenda also provides order and structure. It is usually not effective to try to solve a problem at the time of conflict. The agenda makes students experience a cooling-off period. The agenda also keeps you out of the middle. As we've mentioned before, as issues come up during the week, ask the students to put them on the agenda.

Question: What if students choose a poor solution?

If the class agrees on a solution and later realizes it was a mistake, bring it up at the next meeting and work out another solution. On some occasions you may say, "I can't live with that one." It's best to avoid saying this often, because kids learn so much more by trying out a "bad" suggestion (if it isn't humiliating to another student) for a day or a week and discovering for themselves that it's not a reasonable or workable idea. Another possibility is to role-play the chosen solution, asking the players if they think the suggestion would really help after they've had a chance to experience seeing the solution in action.

Question: What are some of the most common problems found on the agenda at the high school level?

Usually at the high school level the class meeting is used to solve problems between the teachers and the students. The students really appreciate the chance to give input and work with the teacher on a solution. Some of the most common agenda items include (1) sitting where they want, (2) no homework on weekends, (3) getting off task (the teacher usually brings this one up), (4) too much talking, (5) having a hard time paying attention to the teacher after working in small groups, (6) wasting time, and (7) students not showing respect for others.

The problem itself is not of primary importance. Problems provide the opportunity to create a nurturing atmosphere in which students can be empowered with the courage, confidence, and skills they need to be productive, contributing, and happy citizens of the world. When you have this long-range perspective, you won't be discouraged by the ups and downs of class meetings. You may have a lousy class meeting one week and a great one the next. Isn't that what life is all about? What better way to teach kids effective ways to handle their own lives!

Summary of a Question-and-Answer Session

This is a partial transcript of the question-and-answer session during an all-day in-service workshop for five hundred teachers presented by Jane Nelsen in Charlotte, North Carolina.[1] A special part of this workshop was the participation of first-grade teacher Janice Ritter and fourth-grade teacher Kay Rogers, who answered questions about class meetings. Jane visited Janice's and Kay's classrooms several months before the workshop and was thrilled to see students and teachers working together to create an atmosphere of mutual respect—kids were helping each other solve problems and learn life skills, and teachers were giving up their disciplinary hassles.

Jane Nelsen: Today I have with me two teachers from Sharon School. I'd like them to introduce themselves and tell just a little bit about their experience.

Janice Ritter: Last year, when we first started class meetings, my initial reaction was, "Well, this is a terrific idea, but it's not going to fly with first-graders." I didn't think they

---

1. The complete session is part of the six-cassette series entitled *Positive Discipline in the Classroom Featuring Class Meetings,* available from Empowering People Books, Tapes, and Videos, 1-800-456-7770.

could come up with a compliment, let alone solve problems. I went ahead and began the class-meeting process the first week of school, and by December I said, "This is the most wonderful thing that has ever happened to me as a teacher and for the students."

I would like to share a few reasons why I like using class meetings. First of all, you have more children telling you what is going on in your classroom. Also, children sometimes take things said by a peer a lot better than they'll take it from you. Children can say things to each other in a way that reaches children. Adults don't do that very well. I also like the academic skills that grow out of class meetings.

Jane: I hope you all heard that. Say that again.

Janice: The academic skills. As beginning writers, they love to go to that agenda, and it helps their writing skills. I have children who speak in a whisper all day long except when they have something they want to say at the class meeting. Probably the reason I like it the best is because behavior improves.

Jane: A lot of teachers start class meetings to help with discipline problems and to improve behavior. That is an extremely valid reason. However, behavior improvement is a fringe benefit. The main benefit is that it teaches children the Significant Seven [see chapter 1]. That's the foundation that will help them improve their behavior not only now, but all their lives.

Kay Rogers: When our school psychologist gave me a copy of Positive Discipline and wanted me to implement class meetings, my initial reaction was, "Oh no. This is another program that I'm going to have to read, and it's not going to work." There is no one here who could have a more negative attitude than I did. I decided to try it anyway, and after one week I was sold.

Jane: You didn't have a whole month of hell?

Kay: [Laughs] No. After one week of class meetings, it was just wonderful. What it did for me was take care of little nitpicky things that drive teachers crazy. The kids would come to me and say, "Somebody hit me," "Somebody touched me." I would say, "Put it on the agenda." That was what made it worthwhile for me in the beginning. We have worked with class meetings and improved upon them. I have a student teacher who began introducing the idea of Robert's Rules. Not only are they learning problem-solving skills, they are also learning skills that will help them with student government. This has been a tremendous fringe benefit, as well as getting the discipline improved within the classroom.

Jane: I heard that the year before you learned about class meetings, you were asking the psychologist for a lot of help with problem behaviors. She told me she never hears from you anymore and that when she asks if you need anything, you tell her you and the kids are working things out together.

Kay: That's true.

Jane: Kay and Janice will now help me answer some of the questions that were turned in by the faculty members from each school.

Question: Should we post rules in our classroom? And if so, should these be teacher rules, student rules, or a combination of both?

Kay: At the beginning of the year my students and I worked out our own rules together in the classroom. Our school has schoolwide rules, which are also posted in our classroom. They were rules that the student council had come up with.

Jane: What did you find when you asked the kids to come up with rules?

Janice: My students came up with pretty much the same things adults would come up with.

Jane: That's so interesting. I've never been in a classroom yet where there weren't rules posted. But usually they are all neatly printed out by the teacher in advance, so there's no ownership by the kids. What we have found is that the kids will either come up with the same rules or even tougher rules, but then they have ownership and you can label them "We decided" instead of "I decided."

Question: Should a kindergarten classroom meeting include an agenda?

Jane: We had an experience in Elk Grove School District where a group came to visit Project ACCEPT.[2] They were writing a project on decision making and had decided it

---

2. Project ACCEPT (Adlerian Counseling Concepts for Encouraging Parents and Teachers) was a federally funded project directed by Jane Nelsen. The focus of this project was to improve student behavior by training significant adults (parents and teachers) to use Adlerian/Dreikursian methods with children. The main focus for teachers was the use of class meetings. Parents attended parent study groups. After three years of developmental status, the project achieved exemplary status and was awarded dissemination funds for three years. During this three-year period, school districts throughout California used adoption funds for training with their school faculties and parents.

wasn't possible for kids to get involved in decision making until they were in the second grade. But then they watched our kindergarten and our first-grade classes, and they were amazed! They said, "We've got to go back and rewrite the project." Many kindergarten teachers are relieved not to have to deal with tattletale issues. They just say, "Put that on the agenda." Pretty soon the kids get tired of that broken record, so they just put it on the agenda. Half the time they can't remember what their problem was by the time their name comes up on the agenda.

In kindergarten or first grade, it might be okay for children to forget their problems, because once they've had a little time to cool off, it doesn't really matter anyway. But you don't want them to forget too many of their problems, or they won't have the opportunity to work on problem-solving skills.

Question: What do you do when the compliments get monotonous? For example, "I want to compliment you for being my friend," or complimenting the same person every day.

Janice: When that happens, I've done a few things. It happened in the beginning of this year—they were getting very stale. So one day, instead of doing compliments I said, "Today we're going to tell everyone one thing that we're working on." They went around the room and came up with some really good things that they're working on. Whether it was their penmanship or not to talk so much, the rest of the children now had specific things to look for. I don't have to do it that often, but sometimes I find the need to do something like that.

Kay: I find in the older grades that the compliments don't get as stale as often as they do in the lower grades. Students begin to look for academic achievements and socialization skills. I found it helps to pair students. When they sit in pairs, one partner can see what the other partner does.

Jane: Let me see if I understand. They have partners, and they look for things they can compliment their partner on? Do you ever have them change partners?

Kay: Oh, yes! They send their request in writing to me, and every Tuesday is Changing Partners Day.

Jane: What a great idea! This also answers the question about what to do if they're always complimenting the same kid all the time. That's really nice. I hadn't heard of that one before. One that I had heard of is teachers who have kids draw a name out of a hat for a whole week. But I even like this one better. Do they sit by that person for a while?

Kay: They sit by that person for a week.

Jane: Another possibility is to let them get monotonous at first because they're learning the skill. Once they feel comfortable saying, "I want to compliment him for being my friend," you can start teaching them other things. It helps to focus on looking for what a person does—their actions. For example, what do they do to demonstrate their friendship? What specific action would you like to thank them for?

Question: First-grade students seem only to make suggestions that they've heard before. How can we get first-graders to develop solutions that are more appropriate? Are they developmentally ready to create solutions?

Janice: With my first-graders I usually take four suggestions for solutions, and we just talk about those.

Jane: Because your kids are coming up with so many, you have to limit it?

Janice: Yes, more or less, and that's what they can work with. We talk about whether the solutions are appropriate and how they would work to help people. I think you will find a few students who are going to come up with the same suggestions, but you'll have more suggestions once you get started. You will probably see more problem-solving skills developed.

Jane: Part of patience is allowing time. At first the teacher may have to come up with a few suggestions, but the more you learn to keep still and go all the way around the circle, the quicker they're going to start learning what great wisdom and what great ideas they do have. I have found that four-year-olds at family meetings come up with great solutions and great ideas. It's just that we haven't allowed them enough training and experience to know that they can come up with ideas. We're so used to telling kids instead of asking them.

Question: How can we make class meetings more than a tattletale session? It seems that many children thrive on the attention given to them during the session.

Jane: One possibility is to change our feelings about what is a tattletale. What may seem like just tattling to us can be a real problem to students. If we see their concerns as an opportunity to work on solutions instead of tattling, it puts a whole different feeling on their concerns. Usually tattling is, "I want you to punish them," instead of, "This affects me, so how can we solve the problem?" Sometimes teachers like to censor items too much.

Question: What should I do when the same problems come up over and over?

Jane: Sometimes teachers decide, "Well, we've already talked about a problem like that, so let's not do it again." That is missing the whole point of the process of class meetings. The fact that Billy hit Janey is not the same to Susie when Dick hits her. You just keep letting them work on solutions. They'll either get better at coming up with the same solution or come up with different ideas. But the main thing is that they feel listened to, they feel taken seriously, and they use their skills. As long as it affects them, keep letting them work on solutions.

Kay: I've also found that they come up with different solutions for different children, because what works for one doesn't work for all. My students are really beginning to look at the individual rather than just the problem, or to say, "We've already discussed it." They begin to look at what will be effective for this person.

Jane: I'm so glad you said that. That is such an important point! People are unique. They're individuals. What works for one may not work for all. One of the things kids learn in class meetings is that people think differently. They feel differently. They have different ideas. They're not all the same. And so we start learning to respect differences. [See chapter 4.]

Question: What provisions are made for children with severe discipline problems, children with special needs?

Kay: In the two years that I've used class meetings, if I have any discipline problems, I handle them right there. Fortunately, since I've started class meetings I've not had any severe problems.

Jane: Did you think you had severe problems before you had class meetings?

Kay: Yes, and I'm sure I would be having them now if I wasn't doing class meetings. That's one reason I'm so thrilled with class meetings. With the help of the students, we work most things out in our classroom.

Janice: I find the same to be true for me. And I think there are still certain things that you as a teacher have to react to, or if you have a severe discipline problem, maybe you need to refer that child to the proper channels. You would still have to do that even though you're implementing class meetings and trying to solve most of your problems.

Jane: I would like to make just a couple of comments about this. I want to tell you two stories. One is a story about a second-grade boy I'll call Stephen. Because Stephen was a foster child, the teacher asked for help from the Foster Youth Office where I worked. She described Stephen as "a severe discipline problem." His classmates were complaining about all the things he did. I strongly believe that class meetings work, no matter what the severity of the behavior. I knew the best way to help this child was through class meetings, but this teacher didn't know how to do class meetings. I thought, okay, we'll accomplish two things at once. We'll help this child, and we'll teach the class-meeting process to the teacher.

I went into the classroom to demonstrate the class meeting. One rule for class meetings is that usually you do not talk about a child unless that child is there. Once you learn that class meetings can be done in a positive, helpful, encouraging, empowering way, then it's safe for kids to talk about anything together. However, in this case I knew these kids hadn't learned to help each other yet. I knew they'd still have the mentality of ganging up and punishing, so we asked Stephen to leave the room.

The first thing I asked the kids was, "What kind of problems are you having with Stephen?" They listed many complaints. I asked, "Do you have any idea why Stephen might do these things?" They said, "Because he's a bully. Because he's mean." Finally one little kid said, "Maybe it's because he's a foster child." I said, "Do you have any idea what it might feel like to be a foster child?" They said, "Gee, you don't have your family. You don't have your same neighborhood." They started feeling compassion.

Then I said, "How many of you would be willing to help Stephen?" Every hand went up. I said, "Okay, what kinds of things could you do to help Stephen?" They came up with a long list of things on the board: play with him at recess, walk to and from school with him, have lunch with him, and help him with his work. Then I said, "Okay, who would be willing to do each one of these?" I got specific names after each one of their suggestions.

Later I talked to Stephen. "Stephen, we talked about some of the problems you've been having in class. How many kids do you think wanted to help you?" He said, "Probably none of 'em." I said, "Every one." And he said incredulously, "Every one?" He couldn't believe it.

I want to ask you a question. Do you think Stephen's behavior changed when all the kids in that class had changed their way of thinking about him and decided to help? I can guarantee you his behavior changed significantly. When you help kids understand and get into the helping mode rather than hurting, it makes a huge difference. They are able to accomplish more than any one teacher, foster parent, principal, or counselor. The kids are powerful in what they can do to help.

The next story is regarding a class meeting I visited in San Bernardino, California, and a little boy I'll call Phillip. The class discussed four items while I was there. Three of them had to do with Phillip. I asked Phillip, "Do you feel like the kids are helping you?" He just grinned and said, "Yeah, they're helping me." Later the teacher said to me, "Phillip is still the biggest behavior problem in our class, but the kids do try to help him instead of using him as a scapegoat."

Have you noticed that there is always at least one behavior-problem student in every classroom? Is there anybody who does not have one in their classroom? And have you ever noticed that if that child should happen to move, somebody will gladly take his or her place? There is usually one child who decides to be "special" that way. This teacher said, "The thing I like is that even though Phillip still presents most of the problems, the kids really are working with him in ways that are helpful. They really do try to help him instead of always ganging up on him, hurting him, and putting him down."

Question: How do we guide the children into coming up with appropriate solutions?

Janice: I think just by talking it through with them. One of my favorite examples is an experience with a little boy who put things in his mouth all the time. Somebody put that on the agenda because it wasn't safe: he might choke. One student said, "Well, you should put his color on purple." At that time I had a color chart, and when they got down to purple, they would go see the principal. But another said, "Well, that's not going to do him any good because even if he goes to the principal he's still going to put things in his mouth. He's still going to choke." They were thinking things through.

Jane: Because you ask questions like, "How is that going to help?"

Kay: I find virtually the same thing with the fourth-graders. A lot of times I ask them, "Is this reasonable? And is it related to the problem?" And they will go back to it and say, "Oh, well, one of these is not related." And they will discuss which ones are not related and mark them off the list. So, they really do a lot of thinking before they choose a solution.

I've also often found that the first time a problem appears on the agenda, the students' solution to the problem is to stop it. Frequently that's all that's needed. All they need to know is that it is a problem to one of their peers. It is very important to them to have peer approval. If they know that something is displeasing to their peers, many times all they will do is say, "I'll stop it." And it does stop.

Jane: So, in other words, sometimes just a discussion is enough. I really want to emphasize this. So often, people focus too much on consequences or solutions without realizing the power of letting the kids discuss it. [See chapter 9.] After you discuss it you can say, "Okay, if this happens again, it can go on the agenda." But you might be surprised how often it won't happen again.

Asking questions such as, "How will that help?" can be very powerful in teaching kids to consider long-range results. Also, it helps to have the slogan, "We're here to help each other, not to hurt each other." Sometimes you can ask these questions: "How many of you feel like we're coming up with suggestions that are helpful?" "How many of you think we're coming up with suggestions that are hurtful?" A key technique, whenever you see things going wrong, is to ask a question. But ask it both ways: "How many of you think we're being too noisy?" "How many of you think it's quiet enough?" "How many of you think we're being respectful?" "How many of you think we're being disrespectful?" Asking questions invites them to think.

Question: How do we handle children who use the agenda as revenge?

Kay: In the beginning, I did find that the children used the agenda for revenge all the time. So I came up with an agenda box. It has a hole in the top, and they simply put their agenda item in the box. They created a number system. They put a number on the problem then crossed off the number they used so the next person will know which number to use, and we take them in order at the class meeting. So it works beautifully! The children love this, and they're in charge of taking care of it all. I don't do any of it.

Jane: With this system you can keep problems that go in the box in order. That's brilliant!

Janice: I don't notice that first-graders use the agenda for revenge. I just find that they are pretty honest. Usually, a classmate will check on them and say, "She just did that to get back." When I confront them, they'll usually say, "Yeah, I did." I always like to thank them or give them credit for admitting something like that right away.

Jane: Any one of these questions could go on the agenda. You could ask them, "What should we do about people using the agenda for revenge?" They will come up with great answers. But the other thing is that whenever you have a problem, talk about it openly with the kids.

Another way to handle the kids using the agenda for revenge is to say, "I've noticed that we're using the agenda for revenge." Then I would ask some questions like, "How many think that we don't trust each other yet to know that we're here to help each other rather than hurt each other?" Getting the students involved in solutions or a simple discussion is usually enough to stop the revenge.

Question: How do you incorporate other discipline strategies with the Positive Discipline program?

Jane: I have a generic answer for that: It fits any other discipline program that treats kids with dignity and respect, that is not humiliating, that works for solutions rather than blame, and that teaches skills rather than punishment and control. It does not fit discipline programs that are based on a punishment/reward premise. That is a totally opposite premise. Those systems teach adults to be responsible for kids' behavior by catching kids when they're "good" and rewarding them and catching kids when they're "bad" and punishing them. But what happens when the adult is not around? It also is a short-term control, rather than taking a look at what children are feeling and deciding and what kind of skills they are learning for future behavior.

Do you want to make any closing comments? I would like to hear from both of you, just a summarization about what you think about the whole thing.

Kay: Holding regularly scheduled class meetings is one of the most wonderful things that's ever happened to me in my classroom, and my students feel the same way. They love it! They fuss if we miss a class meeting. I have class meetings every day. Once in a while our schedule becomes so hectic we just can't work it in that day, and they really miss it. I find that my classroom operates much more smoothly if we have the opportunity to have the compliments. If we don't have time for anything except compliments, even that makes the day run much more smoothly.

Jane: I'm so glad you mentioned that. So many teachers say that the whole day runs more smoothly when they do have class meetings even if it's only the compliment part.

Janice: I love class meetings. I urge everyone to try it. I never felt comfortable with the discipline program we had when I came into the system. I was so glad to be able to take something that would replace it. I have nothing in place in my classroom now for discipline except class meetings.

We hope this transcript has captured the expertise, positive attitude, and outstanding skills of Janice Ritter and Kay Rogers. We believe their examples will be an inspiration to thousands of teachers who see the potential of class meetings for empowering students and creating a cooperative classroom climate. We hope you, too, will be motivated by their experience to start class meetings and enjoy the fruits of this powerful process for teachers and students alike.

▼

Chapter

11

Positive Discipline Classroom Management Tools

We constantly encourage or discourage those around us and, thereby, contribute materially to their greater or lesser ability to function well.

Rudolf Dreikurs

Students learn both academic and social skills best when classroom management is based on mutual respect. This chapter provides fourteen tools to ensure respectful classroom management throughout the day and is part of the Positive Discipline puzzle. Tool thirteen, Parent/teacher/ student conferences, is such an important tool that we have made it a separate piece of the puzzle. This piece creates a bridge between the school and the home that serves

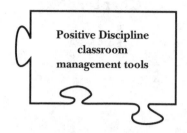

Positive Discipline
classroom
management tools

to help parents be part of the Positive Discipline experience. Every good tool box needs a variety of tools because one tool is not appropriate for every job.

One school principal shared that when a teacher came to her with a complaint about a student, she would open the book to this chapter and go through the headings asking the teacher which Positive Discipline strategies she had tried. This also served as a reminder that there are many possibilities that the teacher could try.

1. Limited Choices

Many difficult problems seem easier to solve when choices are presented. As the teacher, you can help your students succeed by offering them an appropriate choice between at least two acceptable options. The key words are *appropriate* and *acceptable.*

Many times a choice is not appropriate. It's not appropriate, for instance, to give students a choice about whether or not they want to learn to read, go to school, hurt someone else, be in a dangerous situation such as climbing on the roof, and so on. Examples of appropriate limited choices are: "You may read this book or this other book," "It's not okay to hurt your classmate. You can apologize now or take some time to cool off and put this on the agenda for the next class meeting," and "You may stay at recess if you stay off the school roof. If you can't handle that, you can return to the classroom and try again tomorrow."

It's not *appropriate* to give broad choices to younger students, such as, "Where do you want to sit?" or "What do you want to learn?" They need more limited choices, such as, "You may sit at this table or that table," or "We can do our art assignment first or our math assignment. Which do you prefer?" As they get older, the choices you give them can be much broader because their skills at making decisions and dealing with consequences will be better developed. With young students you might say, "Would you like to write a report on a butterfly or a turtle?" With older students you could give a choice such as, "Would you like one week or two weeks to get your report done? You pick the topic."

A choice is acceptable when you are willing to accept either option the student chooses. Don't offer a choice that is not acceptable to you.

2. Classroom Jobs

Assigning classroom jobs—giving students opportunities to contribute in meaningful ways—is one of the best methods of helping kids feel that they belong and are significant. Not only do kids feel better about themselves when they have a job, the teacher doesn't have to do everything!

A simple method for assigning classroom jobs is to brainstorm enough jobs so that every student has one. Suggest that at least one of the jobs is to be job monitor, the person who checks the list each day to see if each job has been done, and if it hasn't, to remind the student who forgot.

Post the list of jobs on a job chart located in a convenient place. Your list might include the following:

Make job chart

Pass out papers

Collect papers

Feed fish

Water plants

Decorate bulletin board

Decorate room

Straighten bookshelves

Restock supplies

Empty pencil sharpener

Be office message monitor

Be line monitor

Be lunchroom monitor

Be playground equipment monitor

Be cleanup monitor

Be morning greeter

Mrs. Petersen's kindergarten class brainstormed jobs for cleanup time and then had fun thinking up silly names for each job. The person who cleans up the constant debris of paper scraps under the tables is called the Tops and Tidy, or T&T. They keep the books they read in individual boxes on their desks, and the person who straightens them up is called the Books and Boxes, or B&B. The person who hands out the papers or other items is called the Table Captain, or TC. The person who sees that the chairs are pushed in is called the Big C. Mrs. Petersen reported, "The room is cleaned up so fast when I say, 'Time to clean the room now.' There are four students at each table, so we have four jobs for clean up time. They rotate each Monday. If someone is absent, the person who had their job the week before does it and their own job also."

Mrs. Traughber's class designed an elaborate chore chart. They made pockets for each job from construction paper. Then each student designed a card with his or her name on it. The first task of the job monitor was to rotate the name cards in the job pockets.

Set up a rotation and switch jobs each week. Sometimes students will prefer to keep the same job for a semester. This is okay only if everyone agrees. You might have a mutiny if one person gets to have the favorite job for long periods.

You may wish to set aside part of each day as job time so that students aren't disruptive when doing their chores. Some jobs may require training, so take time to show a student where the supplies are or how to succeed at the job. Be available at job time to help students who need your assistance.

3. Problem Solving

Often difficulties arise in the classroom that can be easily handled outside the class meeting yet still allow the students, rather than the teacher, to take responsibility for their behavior. Such problems might be solvable by using the Four Problem-Solving Steps. Introduce these steps to the class early in the year and post them in the room.

Four Problem-Solving Steps

1. Ignore it.
   a. Act by walking away instead of reacting.
   b. Take a positive time out for cooling off.
2. Talk it over respectfully with every person involved.
   a. Share how you feel and listen to how others feel.
   b. Take responsibility for what you did to contribute to the problem.

    c. Share what you are willing to do differently.
3. Agree on a win-win solution.
    a. Brainstorm for ideas.
    b. Choose the solution that works for all concerned.
4. Put the problem on the class-meeting agenda.
    a. Consult with each other and learn from the problem.
    b. Brainstorm with more people to generate more ideas.

Choose a problem such as name calling. Divide the class into three groups to plan a role play demonstrating the first three of the Four Problem-Solving Steps to perform before the whole class. Ask that only two or three students from each group be active role players and that the rest be passive participants who notice what they are feeling and thinking during the action. Ask that they create two scenes. The first will be the name calling, or whatever problem you choose. The second will be a scene in which they use the problem-solving steps. Allow ten minutes for planning.

After each scene of each role play, process with the role players how they felt and what they were learning. It is important to ask the passive role players to share what they were feeling, thinking, and learning because this emphasizes that everyone is affected by interactions between people. Then invite comments from the class as to what they learned from watching the role plays. You may want to record their ideas on paper and hang it in the room to reinforce their learning.

When students come to you with a problem, refer them to the Four Problem-Solving Steps chart and ask if they have tried any of the steps. If they haven't tried any, ask which one they would like to try. This keeps you out of the "fix-it" role.

Some classrooms have a problem-solving corner that includes a large poster of the Four Problem-Solving Steps.

Some teachers have the Four Problem-Solving Steps printed on laminated cards and hand them to students who want to use the steps to solve a problem. One school decided to paint the problem-solving steps on a playground bench. When students have a problem on the playground, they are asked to make a choice: to go to the problem-solving bench, to take a positive time out, or to put the problem on the agenda. Students can then choose which of these would help them the most.

4. Follow Through with Dignity and Respect

Positive Discipline in the Classroom offers many other nonpunitive alternatives to help children learn cooperation and social interest. A teacher can decide what he or she will do (instead of what students should do) and can follow through with kind and firm action instead of lectures or punishment. When you use ten words or less that stick to the issue, you avoid lecturing. One word or a pantomimed gesture is best.

When children are young (toddlers to age eight), follow-through is relatively simple. When you say something, mean it. When you mean it, follow through with kindness and firmness. Or, as Dreikurs used to say to parents and teachers, "Shut your mouth and act."

Mrs. Valdez was in the habit of coaxing Jennifer to put her blocks away and come to the reading circle. After learning about follow-through, she decided on a different course of action. The next day at reading time, she went over to Jennifer, took her by the hand, and kindly and firmly led her to the circle. Just before recess Mrs. Valdez asked Jennifer, "What do you need to do before you'll be ready for recess?" Jennifer innocently said, "I don't know." Mrs. Valdez simply pointed to the blocks.

Jennifer went over to the blocks and dallied. She had about half the blocks picked up when the recess bell rang. Mrs. Valdez stopped her at the door, led her back to the block area, and pointed to the blocks. Jennifer picked them up as fast as she could so she wouldn't miss any more recess. Jennifer learned that her manipulative tactics were no longer effective. Mrs. Valdez learned how much easier and effective it was to follow through with very few words than it was to use lectures, threats, and punishment.

If you think your students won't cooperate as readily as Jennifer did, don't be discouraged. If you follow the Four Steps for Effective Follow-Through and avoid the Four Traps That Defeat Effective Follow-Through given below, students will cooperate even when they don't especially want to. They seem to pick up the feeling that what is required is reasonable and that they are being held accountable respectfully.

Follow-through is more effective when children get older if they are more involved in the agreement-making process. The Four Steps for Effective Follow-Through describe this process.

Four Steps for Effective Follow-Through

1. Have a friendly discussion in which everyone gets to voice his or her feelings and thoughts about an issue (during a class meeting or during a conference with one or more students).

2. Brainstorm for possible solutions, and choose one with which both the teacher and the student or students agree.

3. Agree on a specific time deadline (to the minute).

4. Understand your students well enough to know that the deadline may not be met, and simply follow through with your part of the agreement by holding them accountable, as in the above example.

Four Traps That Defeat Effective Follow-Through

1. Expecting kids to have the same priorities as adults.
2. Judging and criticizing instead of sticking to the issue.
3. Not getting (noncoerced) agreements in advance that include a specific deadline or specific action the teacher will take.
4. Not maintaining dignity and respect for the students and yourself while reminding them of their agreement.

Some teachers object to follow-through, saying, "We don't want to have to remind students to keep their agreements. We expect them to be responsible without any reminders from us." We have four questions for these teachers: (1) When you don't take time to remind them with dignity and respect, do you spend time scolding, lecturing, and punishing them for not keeping their agreements? (2) Have you noticed how responsible kids are about keeping agreements that are important to them? (3) Wouldn't you rather do something that is a priority for you than something you don't want to do? (4) What motivates you to do things you don't want to do—respect from others or disrespect? (Even though picking up blocks may not be Jennifer's priority, it is important that she pick up the blocks.)

Follow-through is a gentle way to guide kids to do what needs to be done for their greater benefit or to maintain respect for self and others. Raising and teaching children is not easy. Follow-through can make it easier—and rewarding, too.

Follow-through takes less energy and is much more fun and productive than scolding, lecturing, and punishing. Follow-through helps teachers be proactive and thoughtful instead of reactive and inconsiderate. Follow-through can help you empower students by respecting who they are while teaching them the importance of making a contribution to the classroom. It is an excellent alternative to authoritarian methods or permissiveness. With follow-through you can meet the needs of the situation while maintaining dignity and respect for all concerned. Follow-through is one way to help children learn the life skills they need to feel good about themselves while learning to be contributing members of society.

5. Ask; Don't Tell "What," "Why," and "How"

Too many teachers *tell* students what happened, why it happened, how they should feel about it, and what they should do about it instead of *asking* them what happened, what their perception is of why it happened, how they feel about it, and how they can use that information next time.[1]

When we *tell* instead of *ask*, we discourage students from developing their judgment skills, consequence skills, and accountability skills. We fail to give them the wonderful gift of seeing mistakes as opportunities to learn. Telling instead of asking also teaches them *what* to think instead *how* to think, which is very dangerous in a society filled with peer pressure, cults, and gangs. Whenever you are tempted to *tell*, stop yourself and *ask*.

---

1. For more information, see H. Stephen Glenn and Jane Nelsen, *Raising Self-Reliant Children in a Self-Indulgent World* (Rocklin, Calif.: Prima Publishing, 1989), and Jane Nelsen and H. Stephen Glenn, *Time Out: Abuses and Effective Uses* (Orem, Utah: Empowering People, 1991). Pages 68–72 include an article by a high school principal, Kent Mann, who developed a system based on "what," "why," and "how" questions for working with students sent to his office for behavior problems. Both books are available from Empowering People Books, Tapes, and Videos, 1-800-456-7770.

An eighth-grade teacher wanted to rearrange her room. She started to tell the students what to do and suddenly realized that this would be a great opportunity for them to think through the steps on their own. She asked, "Do you have any ideas for how we could arrange the room so everyone can see each other?" Five or six students had suggestions, and the class voted on one of the ideas.

Out of habit the teacher started to instruct everyone on what to do and realized again that she could ask instead of tell. It took a lot longer than usual to rearrange the room, but the kids got practice in thinking and in being actively involved. Although she was aware of how difficult it is to break the habit of giving all the instructions instead of asking questions, the teacher decided it was worth working on because her students became more engaged than usual, and they all pitched in to rearrange the room instead of leaving the job for a few "regulars."

A word of caution: don't ask unless you are truly interested in students' perceptions and want to help them learn to think and problem solve. Never follow an answer with a lecture. It is not appropriate to tell students that they should be more patient after they tell you that they were angry that they didn't get a turn. Either listen politely or keep asking questions that invite students to come to their own conclusions.

6. Redirection Questions

One of the best ways to redirect behavior is through asking questions related to the behavior you would like to change. For example, when the class is getting too noisy, ask, "How many of you think it's too noisy for people to concentrate? How many do not?" It's important to ask the question both ways in order to allow room for honest responses.

Asking the question is usually enough to invite the students to think about their behavior and what needs to be done. When an atmosphere of mutual respect has been established, the students usually want to cooperate. The question simply helps them become aware of what's needed.

Ask the question while the students keep working. No discussion is needed, but it's interesting to watch how much the situation improves just by asking a redirection question. We watched one teacher use a creative variation of a redirection question by stopping the class in the middle of an activity and saying, "I just have to ask, how many of you want to help Jose with his times tables? Jose, look at all those hands! Pick someone to help you practice your 7s."

7. Doing Nothing (Natural Consequences)

Surprisingly, an effective tool for mutually respectful classroom management is to do nothing and watch to see what happens. An eighth-grade math teacher responded to every little interruption in her classroom. She answered every question, commented on every annoyance, and spent most of her class time putting out fires and getting nowhere. When she heard about the do-nothing idea, she was shocked. It had never occurred to her that she could let some things go by, but she decided to try this new approach.

To her surprise, students usually stopped the disturbing behavior on their own, or classmates asked them to stop. The numerous questions seemed to disappear when she stopped responding to the ones that seemed inappropriate. Later she overheard a student saying, "Don't ask the teacher. She's having a bad day. Maybe I can answer that question."

When she heard the students helping each other, she said, "I'm so happy to see how much you can handle without my involvement. I'm not angry with you or having a bad day, but I really would like to do less reacting and more teaching. How many are willing to help me out?" The entire class raised their hands.

8. Deciding What You Will Do

Will we ever learn that the only behavior we can control is our own? Adults may be able to make children *act* respectfully, but we can't make them *feel* respectful. The best way to encourage them to *feel* respectful is to control our own behavior and be a model of respect for ourselves · and others.

We are disrespectful to kids when we try to control their behavior. An important part of respect and encouragement is honoring a person's right to control his or her own behavior. Even though adults are often disrespectful to children, they insist that children show respect to adults. Does this make sense? Be a model of respect in order to teach respect.

Deciding what to do instead of trying to control others may be a new thought for some teachers. Many teachers have been so busy trying to control their students that they haven't considered the many possibilities for dealing with problems by controlling their own behavior and deciding what they'll do themselves. The following examples should start you thinking creatively.

One teacher got tired of repeating directions all the time. She told the class that she would give directions only once and, if necessary, write them on the board. If someone didn't understand or hear the directions, that was okay; that student could ask a classmate. The teacher was not going to repeat herself. Some students still came to her, but when they did, she simply smiled and shrugged her shoulders. The kids would either begin working or ask others for help.

Another way to decide what you'll do is to make an agreement with a student based on what you are willing to do. For example, you might tell a student, "I'll be available for tutoring every Thursday afternoon from 3:00 to 3:15. If you want my help, I'll be there." If the student doesn't show up and then wants help at a time that is inconvenient for you, say something like, "I'll be available again at 3:00 next Thursday." Avoid the temptation to add a lecture.

At their first class meeting, one seventh-grade class organized the room by putting the tables in a circle and sitting on top of them, even though it was against the teacher's rules. They swung their legs throughout the meeting. Later an aide asked the teacher why she let the students sit on the tables, since it was against the rules. She also wondered if the leg swinging drove the teacher crazy. The teacher replied that she had decided to watch and wait to see if the arrangement created a problem. Even though the leg swinging was a bit annoying, she noticed that the important work was getting done, the students were working on problem solving together, and the meeting proceeded without a hitch. She decided that the leg swinging would not be an issue if she didn't make it one. By the end of the meeting, she didn't even notice whether the students were still swinging their legs.

The next example demonstrates a combination of follow-through and deciding what you will do. Mrs. Adams was having a difficult time with Justin, who continually got out of his seat to ask her questions. Although she tried to answer his questions, she noticed he really seemed to want constant attention. Mrs. Adams tuned into her feelings of irritation and used the Four Mistaken Goals of Behavior chart (see chapter 5) to verify that Justin's goal was Undue Attention. This helped her decide on a plan to encourage him. She said to Justin, "I notice you have a lot of questions. I'm willing to answer three a day. I'll hold up my fingers each time I answer a question, and when three fingers are used up, I won't answer any more questions until tomorrow. You might want to make sure you can't figure out the answer for yourself before you ask me." In this way, Mrs. Adams was weaning Justin from undue attention but still giving him some special attention with their private signal.

Justin acted in his old way on Monday, and Mrs. Adams followed through with firmness and kindness, and no words, after she had answered three questions. On Tuesday he came up to Mrs. Adams's desk twice as many times as usual. (Kids often try harder at first to get the response they used to get before they find a new way of behaving.) She wondered if her idea was going to work, but she remembered that she had decided to try following through for one week. When Justin whined because Mrs. Adams wouldn't answer any more questions, she smiled at him and held up her three fingers. By the fourth day he came up twice, and on Friday he said, "I think I'll only have three questions today. That's enough for next week, too."

Mrs. Adams breathed a sigh of relief and said, "Justin, I'm feeling much better about answering your questions when you don't ask so many. I notice you've been finding many answers for yourself. You are doing a good job."

Justin learned that his teacher means what she says and will follow through with firm and kind action. He also learned that his choices have a related, respectful, and reasonable consequence. Justin has a choice of asking twenty questions and getting three answered or asking three questions. He is learning about responsibility. He is also learning that he's capable of finding some answers for himself. One of the greatest gifts for Justin is the opportunity to learn about treating himself and others with dignity and respect, which the teacher so beautifully demonstrates.

9. Saying "No" with Dignity and Respect

It's okay to say "No." If it's all you *ever* say, that's a problem, but some teachers don't think they have the right to say "No" without lengthy explanations.

One day when a group of students were feeling especially rowdy in a sixth-grade class, they asked their teacher, "Can we take a break and play a game?" The teacher responded, "No." "Why not? That's not fair. Mr. Smith lets his class do it."

This time the teacher said, "Watch my lips. No." "Aw, come on, be a sport. You're so tight." "What part of *no* don't you understand?" "Okay. You're no fun. I guess we have to finish our work." The teacher just smiled. This example could sound disrespectful unless you *feel* the spirit behind it. Some people have wondered why the teacher didn't explain her reasons. Actually it is disrespectful to explain what students already know. These students knew what they needed to do and were trying to manipulate their way out of it. This teacher kindly and firmly avoided manipulation, thus demonstrating kindness and firmness for herself, for the students, and for the needs of the situation.

10. Acting More, Talking Less

You can act instead of talk. Listen to yourself for one day. You might be amazed at how many useless words you speak! If you decide to act more and talk less, your students will begin to notice the difference. Instead of asking over and over for the class to be quiet, wait quietly for them to give you their attention. Flip a light switch if it gets too noisy. One teacher who constantly nagged her students to stay away from the blackboard when they came into the room started walking over to them with her lips closed, gently removing the chalk from their hands, and softly turning them toward their desk. The students were so shocked, they sat down immediately, opened their books, and started working. The teacher was almost as shocked as the class.

The teacher learned to stop saying things she didn't mean. If she meant it, she was prepared to follow through with action instead of words. Since that meant giving an issue her full attention from start to finish, she soon began to ignore minor interruptions and deal with the ones that were really important.

11. Putting Everyone in the Same Boat

Teachers often pick on one student instead of putting everyone in the same boat. It's difficult to really know all the players involved and to pretend to have the ability to be judge, jury, and prosecutor all at once. Some applications of this idea may sound like the following:

> One or two students are whispering while others are doing their work: "Class, it's too noisy in here."
>
> Someone tattles on another student: "I'm sure you two can work it out."
>
> A student grabs another student's book and papers fly all over the room: "Please pick up the papers and get back to work."

If the class responds with, "That's not fair. I wasn't doing anything wrong," or "Teacher, it was Tom, not me," simply say, "I'm not interested in finding fault or pointing fingers but in getting the problem resolved."

Another problem is that many teachers think it's *their* job to fix everything and that *they* are the only ones with good ideas. Another variation of putting everyone in the same boat is to ask those involved in a problem to figure out what to do, and watch their creativity at work.

In one classroom the students were fighting over who got to use the balls at recess. The teacher said, "I'm putting the balls away until all of you figure out a system for sharing without fighting. Let me know when you've worked it out and you can try again." At first the students grumbled, but later three boys announced, "We worked it out. The kids whose last names start with A through M can have the balls on Mondays and Wednesdays, and the N through Z kids can have them on Tuesdays and Thursdays. Friday is free day. We all agreed."

If the students start squabbling again, the teacher can simply say, "Back to the drawing board. The ball-sharing plan seems to be falling apart. Let me know when you're ready to try again, and you can use the balls."

12. Positive Time Out

Time out can be a positive tool—an encouraging and empowering experience for students instead of a punitive and humiliating one.[2] Time out is encouraging when the purpose is to give students a chance to take a break for a short time and try again as soon as they're ready to

---

2. See also Jane Nelsen and H. Stephen Glenn, *Time Out: Abuses and Effective Uses* (Orem, Utah: Empowering People, 1991), available from Empowering People Books, Tapes, and Videos, 1-800-456-7770.

change their behavior. We all have times when, for one reason or another, we don't feel like doing what's required and may choose some form of acting out instead. Time out can be a *cooling-off period.*

Teachers see the value of encouraging time out when they are more concerned with long-range benefits to students than with short-term control at the expense of students. Punitive time out may stop misbehavior for the moment, but the benefits are only short term if the student decides to get even or give up. The key to encouraging, positive time out is the attitude of the teacher and the explanation given to students.

Explain to students that everyone needs time out once in a while, because we all misbehave and make mistakes at times. It can help to have a place to sort out feelings, calm down, and then make a decision about what to do. This is not meant for punishment, but for a time to calm down until you feel better. As soon as you feel better (and you can decide when that is), you can rejoin the group.

Feelings and actions are not the same. What we feel is never inappropriate. What we do often is. "If your behavior is inappropriate (disrespectful to others), I may ask if it would help you to go to the time-out area." Positive time out invites accountability when it is just one option for a student to choose. For example, a teacher could ask, "Which would help you most right now: positive time out, the problem-solving steps, or putting this problem on the agenda?" Some teachers provide a timer for students to set according to how much time they think they'll need to feel better. Other teachers feel comfortable allowing a student as much time as he or she needs.

It is most effective when students help design a positive time-out area. Let them brainstorm ideas for creating an area where they can go when they need time to cool off, calm down, and feel better. They might decide on cushions, a tape player for music, books, and stuffed animals. One high school class designed an area that looked like Hawaii. The whole class created a mural of the ocean, a beach, and palm trees. Students donated two beach chairs, a stuffed dolphin, and sea shells.

An important part of the design of the area is to include guidelines to answer any objections that might be raised by teachers, such as the noise factor or students using the area to avoid work. Students will decide on respectful guidelines when they are given the opportunity to do so. The teacher can give input, such as suggesting that music played on a cassette player with earphones be of a soothing nature and that students can provide a plan to make up work that is missed. Most students decide on a guideline of no more than ten minutes for positive time out. Some teachers allow students to stay as long as they need to, having faith that students will not misuse this privilege. If the privilege is misused, the problem is discussed during a class meeting so solutions can be found.

Some teachers allow students to choose a "listening buddy" to go to time out with them. Students are trained to be listening buddies, which means they just listen or sit quietly to give comfort to a student who may be upset.

People *do* better when they *feel* better. We don't motivate students to do better by making them feel worse through punitive time out. It does not help to tell students, "Go to time out and think about what you did." It is helpful to tell students, "When you are in time out, do something to help you feel better, because I know you will do better when you feel better."

13. Parent/Teacher/Student Conferences

There is one more area where students should be involved but usually are not. We advocate the elimination of par-

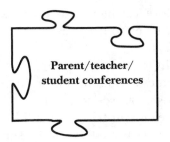

**Parent/teacher/
student conferences**

ent/teacher conferences and suggest instead that you hold parent/teacher/student conferences. Because the purpose of parent/teacher conferences is to encourage students, doesn't it make sense that the student should be present? Don't we teach, "It is not polite to talk about people behind their back?" It is very disrespectful to exclude students from the encouragement process that should be a part of every parent/teacher conference.

To ensure that the parent/teacher/student conference is an encouraging process, we suggest the following agenda.

1. What is going well?
2. What is needed to encourage and support what is going well?
3. In what areas would improvement be beneficial?
4. What is needed to support improvement?

Create an encouragement form in triplicate. List the student's name, the teacher's name, and the parent's name at the top of the form. Give one encouragement form to the student, one to the parent, and keep one for yourself. Ask that each person complete the form before the parent/teacher/student conference.

At the conference, go over each item. Ask the student to share what is going well first. Then each person at the conference can add his or her appreciation for what is going well. Before leaving this area, brainstorm together what is needed to encourage and support continued success.

Also allow the student to share first in the areas of needed improvement. Students know where they need to improve, and this increases accountability instead of the defensiveness they might feel when adults go first. However, it is important for everyone to share his or her perceptions. Again, everyone can brainstorm ways to encourage and support improvement. Let the student choose the suggestions that would be most helpful. When the student and adults disagree about what needs improvement, allow everyone a turn to share his or her reasons while others listen. It is possible that parents and teachers have goals that are not shared by the student. Until goals are shared, the student will defeat any efforts for improvement.

It is possible that adults have unreasonable expectations or that the student has not had the opportunity to think through the long-range results of his or her choices. This might be a good time to help the student explore long-range possibilities with respectful *what* and *how* questions posed in a nonthreatening environment. Adults might benefit from the following point of view.[3]

The book *Soar with Your Strengths* begins with a delightful parable about a duck, a fish, an eagle, an owl, a squirrel, and a rabbit who attend a school with a curriculum that includes running, swimming, tree climbing, jumping, and flying. Of course, all of the animals have strength in at least one of these areas, but they are doomed to failure in other areas. It hits close to home to read about the punishment and discouragement these

---

3. Jane Nelsen, Roslyn Duffy, Linda Escobar, Kate Ortolano, and Debbie Owen-Sohocki, *Positive Discipline in the Classroom: A Teacher's A–Z Guide* (Rocklin, Calif.: Prima, 1996), 61. The references are to Donald O. Clifton and Paula Nelson, *Soar with Your Strengths* (New York: Dell, 1992).

animals encounter when parents and school personnel insist they must do well in every area to "graduate" and become well-rounded animals. A major point of the book is that "excellence can be achieved only by focusing on strengths and *managing* weaknesses, not through the elimination of weakness."

Teach students to manage their weaknesses and soar with their strengths. Students learn mediocrity when their parents and teachers insist they try to earn all As. Sometimes parents and teachers even penalize students by taking away the time they spend on their best subjects (where they feel encouraged) until they do better in their weak areas (where they feel discouraged). Instead, parents and teachers should coach students to spend just enough time on their weak areas to get by and most of their time building on their strengths—so they can soar.

Parents, teachers, and students can all work together to help each other soar. That is what people do when they feel encouraged.

14. Taking Small Steps

Taking small steps is an important classroom management tool. The road to success is one step at a time. If you set your sights too high, you may never start, or you may feel discouraged if everything doesn't happen overnight. If you continue taking small steps, you will move forward, and you and your students will all benefit.

We have discussed many other classroom management tools in other chapters, such as creating routines; following the Three Rs of Recovery; using no words (nonverbal signals), one word, or ten words or less; making sure the message of love gets through; spending special time; encouraging emotional honesty; using encouragement versus punishment and rewards; being kind and firm; seeing mistakes as opportunities to learn; using joint problem solving (in class meetings or one-on-one); using the Four Problem-Solving Steps; using the Wheel of Choice; and understanding the belief behind the behavior. These tools are summarized in a chart on the next page. You may want to keep a copy on your desk and add your own nonpunitive methods that encourage students and promote important life skills.

The point of Positive Discipline classroom management tools and parent/teacher/student conferences is to teach students that mistakes are opportunities to learn, to give them life skills that will serve them when adults are not around, and to help them feel a sense of belonging and significance so they don't feel a need to engage in nonproductive behavior. Hopefully, they also will be encouraging to you.

Positive Discipline Classroom Management Tools
(Tools to avoid punishment, rescuing,
controlling, power struggles, revenge)

Ask "What," "Why," and "How" questions instead of *telling* what, why, and how. Make sure you listen to what the child says.

Limited Choices

Routines: Involve kids in planning

Jobs for a feeling of belonging & significance

Positive Time Out: Let kids help design

The Three Rs of Recovery from Mistakes

See Mistakes As Opportunities for Learning

Act, Don't Talk

One Word

Ten Words

Decide What You Will Do

Two Tongues: If you say it, mean it; and if you mean it, follow through

Put Everyone in the Same Boat

"You kids can figure it out; come back with your plan."

Message of Love

Special Time

Redirection Questions

Emotional Honesty: "I feel _____ because _____ and I wish _____."

Encouragement vs. Praise & Rewards

Nicknames: Give them to the kids with humor and love

Mirror: I notice _____.

Kind and Firm

Go Beyond Consequences/Brainstorm for Solutions

Say "No" (use rarely)

Small Steps

Compliments

Class Meetings

Understand the Belief Behind the Behavior: Use perception modification instead of behavior modification

The Wheel of Choice

Joint Problem Solving with Mutually Agreeable Deadlines

The Four Problem-Solving Steps

Follow Through with Dignity and Respect

Doing Nothing—Allowing Natural Consequences

Teachers Helping Teachers Problem-Solving Steps and Encouragement Meetings

People are interdependent: each of us influences and is influenced.

Rudolf Dreikurs

Have you ever noticed how easy it is to solve someone else's problem? The reason is obvious. We can bring objectivity and perspective to the problems of others when we are not emotionally involved. Have you also noticed that teachers work in isolation and don't like to admit to other teachers that they are having a problem for fear of being judged as inadequate?

The Teachers Helping Teachers Problem-Solving Steps and Encouragement Meetings, another piece of the Positive Discipline puzzle, can change all that. Teachers can realize that they are all in the same boat—that they all have challenges and that they can be great consultants

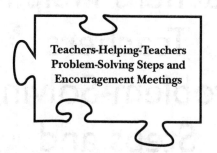

Teachers-Helping-Teachers
Problem-Solving Steps and
Encouragement Meetings

to each other. The Teachers Helping Teachers Problem-Solving Steps and Encouragement Meetings provide a format in which teachers can encourage each other and generate many ideas to encourage students and to solve problems with challenging students.

We offer thorough training in the Teachers Helping Teachers Problem-Solving Steps at our two-day Positive Discipline in the Classroom workshops.[1] However, we believe it is possible for you to learn this process by practicing the steps with two other people three or four times before doing it with a larger group of people. The guidelines for practicing in groups of three can be found at the end of this chapter.

Challenging students are the ones who often push buttons that cause teachers to react instead of act. They are in need of more understanding and more encouragement

---

1. For information on these workshops, please call Jane Nelsen at 1-800-879-0812 or Lynn Lott at (707) 526-3141, ext. 3#.

than the average student—and so is the teacher who is required to meet the challenge.

The Teachers Helping Teachers Problem-Solving Steps serve as an intake, assessment, diagnostic tool, treatment plan, action plan, and encouragement process all rolled into one. These steps are effective because they give teachers practical ideas and skills that work for positive change. Going through the steps with other teachers is fun and nonthreatening. It eliminates the endless analysis that often focuses on causes, blame, and excuses instead of helpful action.

Set Up Regular Encouragement Meetings

Teachers wishing to establish Positive Discipline in their classrooms have found that they need encouragement regularly. When teachers hold weekly, monthly, or bimonthly Encouragement Meetings with each other, they end their isolation, encourage each other, work better with their students, and are more successful in the classroom. Teachers who participate in these meetings say they are well worth the extra time required.

We recommend that each Encouragement Meeting be divided into two parts. In the first part, hold an open discussion dealing with any aspect of the Positive Discipline program. Some teachers call this a book study. They conduct discussions on each chapter of this book, the "yellow book" (the original *Positive Discipline*), *Positive Discipline for Teenagers* (for middle and high school teachers), and many of the other books, tapes, and videos listed in the bibliography. Some teachers use this time to participate in the experiential activities outlined in the *Positive Discipline in the Classroom: Teachers Guide* manual.[2]

---

2. Available through Empowering People Books, Tapes and Videos, 1-800-456-7770.

In the second part of the Encouragement Meetings, usually the last half hour, follow the problem-solving steps presented here to get help with specific problems in class or with a student. During each meeting one teacher can volunteer to share a real problem he or she is having in the classroom. Another teacher can be a facilitator using the following step-by-step approach to come up with a solution that can be tried for one week.

There are two versions of the Teachers Helping Teachers Problem-Solving Steps: (1) a short version that can be transferred to a poster and serve as a guide at a teachers' Encouragement Meeting, and (2) an expanded version, which provides a broader base for the teacher facilitating the problem-solving process at a teacher's meeting. First we will present the expanded version, followed by the short version. The short version can be used as a guide by the person who facilitates the Teachers Helping Teachers Problem-Solving Steps at the regularly scheduled meetings.

Teachers Helping Teachers Problem-Solving Steps (Expanded Version)

▼ 1. *Invite the volunteer teacher to sit next to you and explain the Teachers Helping Teachers Problem-Solving Steps.*

The volunteer teacher sits next to you because he or she is a co-helper with you in this process. This way you can offer encouragement with your friendly energy. Also, you need to be close enough to convey a friendly manner when you need to interrupt.

Explain the Teachers Helping Teachers Problem-Solving Steps by saying directly to the volunteer teacher, "The Teachers Helping Teachers Problem-Solving Steps is a process we can use to solve a school situation that isn't working well. Not only will you get help, but you will help others who watch the process because they will see something of themselves in the situation you describe. They will also be able to use some of the suggestions we create for your situation for their own situations. Thank you for volunteering to be a co-teacher with me in this process."

▼ 2. *Welcome the volunteer teacher and introduce him or her to the others if new to the group. On a flip chart write the volunteer teacher's name, teaching grade level, and number of kids in class. (Birth order of teacher is optional.) Write the challenging student's name, age, and birth order.*

It can be fun to alert the group to some possibilities they could look for based on the birth order of the teacher and the student. For example, if the teacher is the oldest sibling in the family, are perfectionism and bossiness a problem? (Joke with the teacher: "We know you don't have these characteristics, but some other first-born teachers might.") You might ask, "Are you sometimes too hard on yourself when things don't go as well as you would like?" This often helps a first-born person feel understood. For those who are middle born, is trying to save the world a problem? They often see all sides to every issue and get caught up in what's fair. They often work well with rebels and underdogs. For teachers born last in their family, is a lack of order a problem, or are they waiting for someone else to fix things for them? They often allow for lots of creativity. A teacher who is an only child may be similar to an oldest or youngest. Ask only-children teachers if they sometimes have difficulties with students who fight or disagree with each other or borrow items without asking permission.

You can also make some guesses about the student based on birth order. Is a youngest child looking for special service, a middle child looking for a place by being different, an oldest child giving up because he or she can't be first, or an only child having trouble sharing? There may not be time to spend on this issue, but leaders should be aware of it.[3]

▼ 3. *Ask for a brief statement (a one-word or one-sentence headline) of the problem. Ask the group to raise their hands to see if anyone else has ever had a similar problem. This is important because seeing those hands helps the volunteer know he or she is not alone.*

In this step you are looking for a general idea of the problem, not the details. Sometimes a teacher may give too much detail. Interrupt and say, "If you could describe the problem in one word or one sentence, what would it be?"

It's important to ask the group if they have a similar problem. It is very encouraging for the teacher not to feel alone or inadequate by knowing others are or have been in the same boat.

▼ 4. *Ask the teacher to describe the last time the problem occurred in enough detail and dialogue (like a movie script) so that the group can get an idea of how to role-play the situation. If the volunteer needs help describing the situation, ask, "What did you do?" "What did the student do?" "Then what happened?" "What happened next?"*

In this step you are looking for a specific example of the problem. Unless you focus on one incident, you, the teacher, and everyone involved will become overwhelmed and leave without satisfactory help. One episode represents a microcosm of what occurs between this teacher and student. Focusing on and understanding the single incident will help other teachers with similar situations.

Specifics are important because they help you find more clues about the mistaken goal. What the teacher did and the student's response to what the teacher did provide more clues about the mistaken goal and thus the reason for the student's misbehavior. For example, if

---

3. See chapter 3 in *Positive Discipline* (the yellow book; New York: Ballantine, revised edition, 1996) for more information on birth order.

the student stops the behavior for a while in response to
what the teacher did but starts up again a few hours or
days later, the mistaken goal is probably undue attention.
If the student resists cooperation (actively or passively),
the goal is probably power.

Ask for a description of the last time the problem
occurred that includes details and dialogue for role players. This helps the teacher focus on the incident instead of
telling stories about background and causes. Background
details are a distraction to this process. Those details could
be discussed forever without focusing on solutions. Sticking to the steps as outlined keeps the focus on finding a
solution for a specific incident that brings clarity to
the whole.

▼ 5. *Ask the teacher, "How did you feel?" (If the volunteer has
difficulty expressing a one-word feeling, refer him or her to the
second column of the Mistaken Goal Chart and ask him or her
to choose the group of feelings that fits.) Ask the group, "How
many of you have ever felt that way?" (Again, this is important so
that the volunteer knows that he or she is not alone.)*

Most people are not used to identifying their feelings.
Explain that it takes only one word to describe a feeling. If
the teacher is going on and on about what he or she
thinks instead of what he or she feels, or if he or she comes
up with a vague feeling such as "frustrated," use the Mistaken Goal Chart (page 73) and ask the teacher to find
a feeling in the second column that comes closest to
describing his or her own.

Check with the group to see if they have felt the same
so that the teacher is encouraged by knowing others have
shared the feeling.

▼ 6. *Based on the feeling expressed, guess the student's mistaken
goal using the Mistaken Goal Chart.*

It is important for the teacher to express feelings, because they give us clues about the belief behind the student's behavior, which we call the student's mistaken goal.

If appropriate you can explain to the group, "What the teacher feels gives us the clue to the student's mistaken goal. For example, if the teacher feels annoyed, this is a clue that the student's mistaken goal is Undue Attention." Some people get this confused and think you have to know what the *student* feels in order to understand his or her goal.

Don't spend a lot of time trying to figure out the goal, especially if the conversation turns to analysis. Say, "Let's see what more information we get from the role play." Even if you never know for sure what the mistaken goal is, people will get help from role-playing and brainstorming.

▼ 7. *Ask, "Would you be willing to try something else that would be more effective?"*

This question is important to verify, clarify, and substantiate a commitment to trying something else. Help the teacher conclude from known results that more of the same won't produce different results by joking, "Have you heard the definition of insanity? Doing the same thing over and over and expecting a different result. Only adults do that. Kids are smart enough to keep doing what works for them or to try something else if what they do doesn't work."

Once in awhile a teacher might say something like, "I have already tried everything." It is extremely rare, but if a teacher does not show a willingness to try something else, do not go further. Thank him or her for sharing this much and stop the process.

▼ 8. *Set up and perform a role play of the scene that was described. (Remember that the role play need not take longer that one or two minutes to give all the information needed.)*

Use your intuition to determine which role the teacher should play in order to learn the most. As a general rule it's helpful for the teacher to role-play the student, to "get into the student's world." Sometimes a teacher might be feeling vulnerable, and it might be best for the teacher to watch the role play instead. Later, when role-playing the suggested solution, it's usually best to have the teacher play him- or herself to practice the skill of the new suggestion. Again, you might feel it best for the teacher to watch or experience the student's reaction to the suggestion.

Assign someone to play each part. Have four to six people represent students in the classroom. Tell them to start with the dialogue they heard during the description of the problem.

Some facilitators are afraid that people might object to role-playing, and some people do. But a facilitator who is confident about the value of role playing won't be discouraged by the resistance. Proceed to set up the role play with confidence. When you ask for volunteers to play roles, be quiet and wait. Someone will fill the void of silence and volunteer. You might joke with them in your own way, or say, "I feel resistance. It reminds me of my resistance before I found out how valuable this is and how much fun it can be. Okay, who are the brave souls who are going to jump in and help me show how much fun this is?"

Set up the room to represent the real situation. Are the desks in rows or groupings? Is the teacher in the front of the room or somewhere else? It's important to have a few people represent the rest of the kids in the class, because they'll show how one person's behavior affects everyone else.

To get the role play started, remind someone of their opening line, or ask the volunteer teacher to remind someone of an opening line.

▼ 9. *Process the role play by asking players to share feelings and decisions.*

Stop the players as soon as you think they've had enough time to experience feelings and decisions (usually less than a minute or two). Ask the players, one at a time, what they were feeling and what they were deciding as the people they were playing. This information sheds more light on the problem, and the processing serves as a debriefing for role players who may be left with a lot of stirred-up feelings they need to express. Asking the students what they are deciding helps teachers see the long-range results of their actions instead of just the immediate result. Remember, feelings can usually be expressed in one word.

▼ 10. *Brainstorm with the group for possible solutions the teacher could try. (Be sure every suggestion is written down.)*

Ask a volunteer to write down all suggestions on the flip chart. Ask everyone in the group to refer to the alternative column on the Mistaken Goal Chart (page 73) for suggestions or to make suggestions from their personal experience.

Brainstorming allows each person to participate. It helps people accept and value how easy it can be to solve other people's problems. When it's someone else's problem, we are not emotionally involved, so we have objectivity and perspective. Once we accept this, we can appreciate the value of being consultants to each other instead of thinking we should be able to solve all our own problems—or that we are failures if we even admit we have a problem.

Encourage the group to think of as many alternatives as possible. Make it safe for them to make suggestions by respecting and writing down each suggestion on the flip chart. This is not a time for discussion or asking questions of the volunteer teacher, nor is it time to analyze any of the suggestions with the volunteer teacher.

Suggestions will improve as teachers learn to use more of the tools described in this book. Do not censor negative suggestions. If a negative suggestion is chosen, be sure the teacher role-plays the student so that he or she can experience what the student might feel and decide in response to that suggestion.

▼ 11. *Ask the teacher to choose a suggestion to try for one week.*

Read aloud all the suggestions, and then ask the volunteer to choose one he or she would be willing to try. Once in a while a teacher will say, "I've already tried all of them." Say something like, "Sounds like you really care and are trying every thing you can think of. Would you be willing to pick one you have already tried, and we'll see what we can learn from the role play about why it isn't working?"

▼ 12. *Role-play the chosen suggestion so the teacher can practice.*

In most cases it is best to have the teacher play him- or herself. Some teachers prefer just to watch, while some prefer to play the student to get that perspective. This is a good chance for the teacher to practice the chosen suggestion. Many times we'll have a good idea, but when we try to apply it, we incorporate some of our old habits (such as lecturing, controlling, throwing in a little humiliation) and then wonder why it didn't work. All this will come out in the role play, and those watching will also gain some insight about why some of the things they do may not be working.

If the person role-playing does start lecturing or doing something other than the chosen suggestion, it is okay to interrupt and say, "Excuse me. What did you say you were going to do?" This almost always causes laughter from the role players and others as everyone sees how easy it is to get sidetracked into old habits. That is one reason why it is so important to role-play the suggestion.

If the chosen suggestion is a negative one, the role play will demonstrate why it doesn't work when you process the student's feelings and decisions. It is important to ask all role players what they were feeling and deciding in order to learn how a situation affects everyone. Finding out that a chosen suggestion won't work does not mean the time has been wasted. Everyone will learn many valuable things during the process.

▼ 13. *Ask for the teacher's commitment to try the suggestion for one week and to report back to the group at the following meeting.*

Let the teacher know how important it is for the group to hear the results of his or her efforts so everyone can know how their suggestions work in the real world. (We recommend regularly scheduled meetings for teachers, no less than once a month and preferably once a week while they are learning these new skills.)

If the suggestion did not produce positive results in the role play, ask the teacher what he or she learned from it. Ask if he or she would be willing to see what happens based on what was learned, and ask him or her to report back to the group next week. Let everyone know that part of the process is the learning that takes place at a subconscious level. Many teachers find that they do something from their own creativity the next time they encounter the problem because of what they learned during the Teachers Helping Teachers Problem-Solving Steps.

▼ 14. *Ask the group for appreciations for the volunteer teacher.*

What help did you get for yourself by watching this? What did you see that you appreciate about the volunteer? What ideas did you see that you could use? This is the time to give back to the volunteer by telling him or her what this experience gave to you. Appreciations may sound like this: "I learned _____," "I felt _____," "I have the same problem, so now I can try _____," "I know how hard it is to share _____," or "Thank you for _____."

Once teachers have become familiar with the expanded version, the short version provides an outline of the steps to be followed. Teachers may want to rotate the facilitator position so that everyone has an equal opportunity to have fun making mistakes while learning. The facilitator and every member of the group should have a copy of the Mistaken Goal Chart so they can refer to it when guessing the mistaken goal and when brainstorming for suggestions.

Teachers Helping Teachers
Problem-Solving Steps (Short Version)

1. Invite the volunteer teacher to sit next to you and explain the Teachers Helping Teachers Problem-Solving Steps.

2. Welcome the volunteer teacher and introduce him or her to the others if new to the group. On a flip chart write the volunteer teacher's name, teaching grade level, and number of kids in class. (Birth order of teacher is optional.) Write the challenging student's name, age, and birth order.

3. Ask for a brief statement (a one-word or one-sentence headline) of the problem. Ask the group to raise their hands to see if anyone else has ever had a similar problem. This is important because seeing those hands helps the volunteer know he or she is not alone.

4. Ask the teacher to describe the last time the problem occurred in enough detail and dialogue (like a movie script) so that the group can get an idea of how to role-play the situation. If the volunteer needs help describing the situation, ask, "What did you do?" "What did the student do?" "Then what happened?" "What happened next?"

5. Ask the teacher, "How did you feel?" (If the volunteer has difficulty expressing a one-word feeling, refer him or her to the second column of the Mistaken Goal Chart and ask him or her to choose the group of feelings that fits.) Ask the group, "How many of you have ever felt that way?" (Again, this is important so that the volunteer knows that he or she is not alone.)

6. Based on the feeling expressed, guess the student's mistaken goal using the Mistaken Goal Chart.

7. Ask, "Would you be willing to try something else that would be more effective?"

8. Set up and perform a role play of the scene that was described. (Remember that the role play need not take

longer that one or two minutes to give all the information needed.)

9. Process the role play by asking players to share feelings and decisions.

10. Brainstorm with the group for possible solutions the teacher could try. (Be sure every suggestion is written down.)

11. Ask the teacher to choose a suggestion to try for one week.

12. Role-play the chosen suggestion so the teacher can practice.

13. Ask for the teacher's commitment to try the suggestion for one week and to report back to the group at the following meeting.

14. Ask the group for appreciations for the volunteer teacher.

At the next teacher Encouragement Meeting, allow time for the volunteer to share what happened. Remember, this is not about perfection. It is about learning from successes and failures. Do not think of a failure as a bad experience but as an opportunity for learning.

When practicing the Teachers Helping Teachers Problem-Solving Steps in groups of three (we call these ABC groups) and later with a larger group, trust the process. If you stick to the steps, you will find encouragement and greater understanding of yourself and your students even if you don't find a "magic" solution. However, the solutions teachers find in this process often do seem like magic. It can seem like magic when teachers gain insight and/or ideas from their colleagues that they could not see before going through this process.

ABC Groups: Job Descriptions

Each person in the group can take a turn in each of the roles (jobs) required for practicing the Teachers Helping Teachers Problem-Solving Steps.

A. Volunteer

1. Present a real, first-party problem. The problem could involve a student, a colleague, your own child, your spouse, your boss, or a friend. This process is effective with any relationship concern.

2. Relax and allow the facilitator to lead you through the fourteen steps.

3. Participate in the role play both times. (When there are only three people, you do not have the luxury of watching.)

4. Join in the brainstorming for suggestions. (In larger groups, the volunteer usually just listens while others brainstorm.)

B. Facilitator

1. Lead the volunteer through the steps.

2. Participate in the role play if needed. (If it is a classroom situation, you might represent other students in the class or any other role that is required.)

3. Join in the brainstorming for suggestions.

C. Observer

1. Record names as required in step two of the fourteen steps, and record the brainstorm ideas.

2. Participate in the role play.

3. Join in the brainstorming for suggestions.

4. Monitor the steps so you can gently interrupt the facilitator if he or she gets off track.

The job of interrupting is an important one, since sticking to the steps is essential in this process. Interrupting can be done with dignity and respect: "Excuse me. I think we are off track," "Excuse me, I think you skipped a step," or "Whoops, you forgot to ask others if they have ever felt the same."

As we teach the problem-solving steps to ABC groups in our workshops, we have discovered several problems that occur over and over. It may help if we emphasize these and if the observer makes a special point to interrupt when they happen.

Typical Problems of ABC Groups

1. Facilitators don't follow the outline and stick to the steps.

2. People get caught up in the story. It is important to stick to one time when the problem occurred. Background information is not necessary for this process.

3. The group members analyze, question, and evaluate information.

4. The group forgets to suggest some of the tools presented in the book or from the last column of the Mistaken Goal Chart. Each person in the group should have a copy of the Mistaken Goal Chart (page 73) and a copy of the Positive Discipline Classroom Management Tools (page 183) to help generate brainstorming ideas. Of course, once the brainstorm energy kicks in there will be other creative ideas from the group.

5. The group skips steps, such as the role playing or appreciations. Every step is important in small groups or large.

Even teachers who have been reluctant to try the Teachers Helping Teachers Problem-Solving Steps have been impressed with the encouragement and help they received through this process. They have been surprised at how much understanding they gained by role-playing the student (or others) to "get inside their shoes." They have enjoyed the encouragement from their colleagues and have acquired many ideas they can use to encourage their students.

The encouragement process is ongoing. As teachers continue to encourage each other—especially with specific and practical ideas they can use—they will encourage their students. Classrooms will provide the kind of positive environment that enhances learning—both academic and social. Encouragement is the key.

▼

Appendix

When Logical Consequences Are Appropriate

Even though logical consequences are usually misused, they can be used in an encouraging and empowering manner. Logical consequences can be appropriate when all the pitfalls are avoided and the focus is on helping students learn accountability for their choices in a nurturing environment.

Here are nine suggestions for ensuring that consequences are not misunderstood and are not disguised punishment.

1. If it isn't obvious, it isn't logical. One of the most popular questions we hear is, "What would be the logical consequence for _____?" The answer is, "If a consequence is not obvious, then a consequence probably is not logical or appropriate." It is also possible that you are unable to think of something logical because you may be feeling

punitive or may not have had enough practice thinking logically. For example, it is obvious that if a child draws on a wall or a desk, it would be related, respectful, and reasonable for that child to clean the wall or desk (or, if very young, at least help clean the wall or desk). If we have to struggle to identify a logical consequence, it's a clue that we might be headed for a punishment instead of a solution. Notice that this example shows that appropriate consequences help solve the problem instead of merely punishing the child. The graffiti gets cleaned up.

2. Make sure consequences are helpful, not hurtful. The poster (see figure 4.2) "We are here to help each other" is a good reminder. Some people get fixated on consequences and forget the ultimate goal of helping or believe that children have to suffer to learn. For example, an apology is a logical consequence that might help both people feel better. Cleaning up a mess can help students develop social interest and takes care of the mess problem. However, both of these consequences become hurtful if the students who could benefit are blamed or shamed. We help students maintain accountability and integrity when they are involved in the creation and choosing of solutions. In other words, an attitude of respect is essential. It is also essential to remember and teach that mistakes are wonderful opportunities to learn.

3. It is a mistake to think there must be a logical consequence for every behavior or to solve every problem. Put less emphasis on consequences and more emphasis on solving the problem. Focusing on problem solving helps you get out of a punitive, retaliatory mentality.

4. Involve the students in creating logical consequences. Young people are our greatest untapped resource. They have a wealth of wisdom and talent for solving problems, and numerous benefits result when they become involved. When kids participate in creating con-

sequences, not only do they use and strengthen their skills, they are also more likely to keep agreements because they have ownership. They develop self-confidence and self-esteem when they are listened to, taken seriously, and valued for their contributions. Because they feel part of the classroom community, they have less motivation to misbehave and are more willing to work on solutions to problems.

5. Focus on the future instead of the past. Rather than focusing on making students "pay" for what they've done, look for solutions that will help them learn for the future. One fifth-grade class was trying to help a student who was unhappy about another student who scribbled on his spelling test while correcting it. One suggestion was that the scribbler spend half an hour in study hall; another was to give the scribbler an extra piece of paper to scribble on while correcting tests. The first suggestion focuses on making the scribbler pay for the mistake, while the second focuses on helping him solve the problem in the future.

6. Make the opportunity-responsibility-consequence connection. Every opportunity has a related responsibility. The obvious consequence for not wanting the responsibility is to lose the opportunity. For instance, kids have the opportunity to use the playground during recess. The related responsibility is to treat the equipment and other people with respect. When people or things are treated disrespectfully, the logical consequence is losing the opportunity of using the playground for a while. To instill a sense of responsibility, accountability, and empowerment in a student who has acted disrespectfully, say, "You decide how much time you think you need to cool off and calm down. Let me know when you are ready to use the playground respectfully." Consequences are effective only if they are enforced respectfully and students are given

another opportunity as soon as they are ready for the responsibility.

7. Give students choices about what might help them the most. When students are disrespectful on the playground, some schools offer three choices: "Which would help you the most right now: to put this problem on the agenda, to go to the problem-solving area with the other student, or to go to the positive time out area?" The student or students will then choose the one that will be most helpful. This increases accountability and responsibility. The immediate problem is dissipated. If the student chooses the problem-solving area or the class-meeting agenda, a solution will be found later. If the student chooses positive time out, he or she can come back when ready–which means he or she has decided to change his or her behavior. Again, the focus is on solutions.

Another possibility is to give yard duty personnel a laminated copy of the Wheel of Choice (see chapter 7). When problems are encountered, the yard duty person could intercede by showing the wheel to students who are having a problem and asking them to choose the solution they would like to try. A fun way to distract students from strong emotions is to make a game of it. Add a spinner to the wheel and ask students to flick the spinner and see if it lands on a solution that would work for them. If it doesn't, they can choose a solution that would work for them, or they can keep spinning until the spinner stops on a solution they like.

8. Avoid piggybacking. Piggybacking is adding something to the consequence that isn't necessary and is actually hurtful, such as, "Maybe this will teach you!" or "You can just sit there and think about what you did!" It's easy to make the mistake of turning consequences into punishment by piggybacking because it's based on the belief that in order to make people do better, first we have to make them feel worse.

Adults often use piggybacking to add punishment to something that would otherwise be a natural or logical consequence or a solution that would work without punishment. In one class, two students agreed to a suggestion to solve their problem of being late after recess. Instead of letting them try out their solution, the teacher wanted to solve a problem that hadn't even occurred yet. She asked the class to discuss what the consequence would be if the boys were late again. The class seemed to pick up her piggybacking mentality. They came up with several suggestions, but instead of being helpful, most of their solutions sounded punitive. They voted on sending the two boys to the principal.

Later that day the teacher came across the two boys, who were in tears because they thought being sent to the principal was unfair. They felt ganged up on and that they were treated disrespectfully. They were right. She told the boys that she had made a mistake, explaining what it was. Then she asked if they would be willing to let her try again at the next class meeting so she could correct her mistake. The boys stopped crying and said, "Okay, but do we have to go to the principal?" "No," she said, "just stick with your choice to play closer to the bell. If that doesn't work, we can try again at the class meeting to come up with another plan, but one that isn't hurtful. Okay?"

9. Plan solutions in advance. One way to avoid the feeling of punishment is to get students involved in deciding on solutions in advance. During a class meeting or a problem-solving session, ask the students for help in determining what would help them learn. For example, "What do you think would be a solution to help classmates remember to use the school equipment respectfully?" If students aren't involved in the planning, at least give them advance notice. For instance, inform them that people who abuse the special resource display area may be asked to leave the area until they are ready to use the area respectfully again.

Even with these guidelines, it is important to remember that logical consequences are rarely necessary and are only one possibility. Looking for solutions is more effective in most situations.

This does not mean that students should not learn about logical consequences. However, logical consequences are more appropriately understood when taught in a context of personal responsibility. Teachers often object, "But students have to experience the consequences of their choices in real life. For example, if they speed they may get a ticket or if they steal they may go to jail." This is true. This is why it is important to help students understand the consequences of their choices based on a foundation of personal responsibility and sound judgment skills. They learn neither responsibility nor judgment skills in an environment of punishment. Yes, tickets and jail are punishment—something we want to help students learn to avoid.

Teaching Students About Logical Consequences

Teach students about consequences by helping them understand the consequences of their choices. They can then explore alternatives.

Activity: Ask your students what happens when they:

1. Don't do their homework
2. Hit others
3. Call people names
4. Are tardy for school or after recess
5. Shove in line
6. Get a poor grade

Choose one subject at a time. Write their responses on the blackboard. Many of their responses will include what others will do to them in the form of punishment or retaliation.

Next ask them what would happen to them if no one else did anything to them. What would the results of their actions be? For example, what is the long-range result for them if they don't do their homework? (They might fail the test.) What will happen if they hit others, call people names, or shove in line? (They might hurt others, lose their friends, or miss out on learning to solve problems respectfully.) What will happen if they are tardy? (They might miss something important or disrupt the class.) By the way, if they wouldn't fail a test or miss something important by not doing their homework or being tardy, perhaps adults need to look at why they make such an issue of these things.

Accountability means that people take responsibility for their actions instead of blaming others. The next part of this activity is to ask the students to explore alternatives (solutions) that would help people make choices that would be of benefit to them. Ask them, "If you get a poor grade, is that your responsibility or the teacher's? Does the teacher give you a poor grade, or do you earn a poor grade? If you want a good grade, what do you need to do?"

The last question to ask is, "What would help you be willing to accept responsibility for your choices: punishment or exploring solutions? Why?" Don't be surprised if some students say punishment helps them. Many are used to external motivation. You may need to ask other questions to help them explore the difference between doing something because they see the value of it to themselves or for others and doing something because someone else makes them.

Helping Students Understand the Consequences of Their Choices

The one area in which logical consequences could be the most valid is helping students understand the logical consequences of their choices. There are two reasons why adults usually are not successful mentors in this process: (1) instead of helping students explore their choices by using "what" and "how" questions in a friendly manner, adults usually engage in lectures designed to blame and shame, and (2) adults often want to make students pay for what they have done instead of to help them learn from what they have done.

It is time for a major shift in our thinking about logical consequences. Children will be willing to explore the consequences of their choices only when adults create a safe environment for them to do so. Positive Discipline methods can create that safe environment.

▼

Bibliography

Adler, Alfred. *Cooperation Between the Sexes*. New York: Anchor Books, 1978.

———. *Social Interest*. New York: Capricorn Books, 1964.

———. *Superiority and Social Interest*. Evanston, IL: Northwestern University Press, 1964.

———. *What Life Should Mean to You*. New York: Capricorn Books, 1958.

Albert, Linda. *Coping with Kids*. New York: E. P. Dutton, 1982.

Allred, G. Hugh. *How to Strengthen Your Marriage and Family*. Provo, UT: Brigham Young University Press, 1976.

———. *Mission for Mother: Guiding the Child*. Salt Lake City, UT: Book Crafts, 1968.

Ansbacher, Heinz and Rowena. *The Individual Psychology of Alfred Adler*. New York: Harper Torchbooks, 1964.

Bayard, Robert and Jean. *How to Deal with Your Acting Up Teenager*. San Jose, CA: The Accord Press, 1981.

Beecher, Willard and Marguerite. *Beyond Success and Failure*. New York: Pocket Books, 1966.

Bettner, Betty Lou, and Amy Lew. *Raising Kids Who Can*. New York, HarperCollins, 1992.

Christianson, Oscar. *Adlerian Family Counseling*. Minneapolis, MN: Educational Media Corp., 1983.

Corsini, Raymond, and Genevieve Painter. *The Practical Parent*. New York: Harper and Row, 1975.

Dinkmeyer, Don, and Rudolf Dreikurs. *Encouraging Children to Learn: The Encouragement Process*. Englewood Cliffs, NJ: Prentice-Hall, 1963.

Dinkmeyer, Don, and Gary McKay. *Parents Handbook: Systematic Training for Effective Parenting*, 3rd edition. Circle Pines, MN: American Guidance Service, Inc., 1989.

———. *Raising a Responsible Child*. New York: Simon & Schuster, 1978.

Dinkmeyer, Don, and W. L. Pew. *Adlerian Counseling and Psychotherapy*. Monterey, CA: Brooks/Cole Publishing, 1979.

BIBLIOGRAPHY

Dreikurs, Rudolf. *Psychology in the Classroom.* New York: Harper and Row, 1966.

———. *Social Equality: The Challenge of Today.* Chicago: Contemporary Books, Inc., 1971.

Dreikurs, Rudolf, Raymond Corsini, and S. Gould. *Family Council.* Chicago: Henry Regnery, 1974.

Dreikurs, Rudolf, Bernice Grunwald, and Floyd Pepper. *Maintaining Sanity in the Classroom.* New York: Harper and Row, 1971.

Dreikurs, Rudolf, and V. Soltz. *Children: The Challenge.* New York: Dutton, 1964.

Glenn, H. Stephen. *Developing Capable People* (audio tape set). Orem, UT: Empowering People Books, Tapes & Videos. (1-800-456-7770)

———. *Developing Capable People* (video tape set). Orem, UT: Empowering People Books, Tapes & Videos. (1-800-456-7770)

———. *Developing Healthy Self-Esteem* (audio tape). Orem, UT: Empowering People Books, Tapes & Videos, 1989. (1-800-456-7770)

———. *Developing Healthy Self-Esteem* (video tape). Orem, UT: Empowering People Books, Tapes & Videos, 1989. (1-800-456-7770)

———. *Involving and Motivating People* (audio tape). Orem, UT: Empowering People Books, Tapes & Videos, 1986. (1-800-456-7770)

———. *Teachers Who Make a Difference* (audio tape). Orem, UT: Empowering People Books, Tapes & Videos, 1989. (1-800-456-7770)

———. *Teachers Who Make a Difference* (video tape). Orem, UT: Empowering People Books, Tapes & Videos, 1989. (1-800-456-7770)

Glenn, H. Stephen, and Jane Nelsen. *Raising Self-Reliant Children in a Self-Indulgent World.* Rocklin, CA: Prima Publishing, 1988.

Kvols-Riedler, Bill and Kathy. *Redirecting Children's Misbehavior.* Boulder, CO: R.D.I.C. Publications,

Lott, Lynn, and Riki Intner. *The Family That Works Together.* . . . Rocklin, CA: Prima Publishing, 1995.

Lott, Lynn, Marilyn Matulich Kentz, and Dru West. *To Know Me Is to Love Me.* Orem, UT: Empowering People Books, Tapes & Videos, 1990. (1-800-456-7770)

Lott, Lynn, and Jane Nelsen. *Teaching Parenting the Positive Discipline Way* (a manual). Orem, UT: Empowering People Books, Tapes & Videos, 1990. (1-800-456-7770)

Lott, Lynn, and Dru West. *Together and Liking It.* Orem, UT: Empowering People Books, Tapes & Videos, 1990. (1-800-456-7770)

Manaster, Guy J., and Raymond Corsini. *Individual Psychology.* Itasca, IL: F. E. Peacock Publishers, Inc., 1982.

Nelsen, Jane. *Positive Discipline.* New York: Ballantine Books, 1981, 1987, 1996.

BIBLIOGRAPHY

———. *Positive Discipline* (audio tape). Orem, UT: Empowering People Books, Tapes & Videos, 1988. (1-800-456-7770)

———. *Positive Discipline* (video tape set). Orem, UT: Empowering People Books, Tapes & Videos, 1988. (1-800-456-7770)

———. *Understanding: Eliminating Stress and Finding Serenity in Life and Relationships.* Rocklin, CA: Prima Publishing, 1988, 1997.

Nelsen, Jane, Roslyn Duffy, and Cheryl Erwin. *Positive Discipline for Preschoolers.* Rocklin, CA: Prima Publishing, 1994.

Nelsen, Jane, Roslyn Duffy, Linda Escobar, Kate Ortolano, and Debbie Owen-Sohocki. *Positive Discipline: A Teacher's A-Z Guide.* Rocklin, CA: Prima Publishing, 1996.

Nelsen, Jane, Cheryl Erwin, and Carol Delzer. *Positive Discipline for Single Parents.* Rocklin, CA: Prima Publishing, 1993.

Nelsen, Jane, and H. Stephen Glenn. *Time Out: Abuses and Effective Uses.* Orem, UT: Empowering People Books, Tapes & Videos, 1992. (1-800-456-7770)

Nelsen, Jane, Riki Intner, and Lynn Lott. *Positive Discipline for Parenting in Recovery* (previously published as Clean and Sober Parenting). Rocklin, CA: Prima Publishing, 1996.

Nelsen, Jane, and Lynn Lott. *Positive Discipline for Teenagers.* Rocklin, CA: Prima Publishing, 1994.

Nelsen, Jane, Lynn Lott, and H. Stephen Glenn. *Positive Discipline: A–Z.* Rocklin, CA: Prima Publishing, 1993.

———. *Positive Discipline in the Classroom.* Rocklin, CA: Prima Publishing, 1993.

Pew, W. L., and J. Terner. *Courage to Be Imperfect.* New York: Hawthorn Books, 1978.

Smith, Manuel J. *When I Say No I Feel Guilty.* New York: The Dial Press, 1975.

The Video Journal of Education. "Positive Discipline in the Classroom." Program One: "A Foundation for Positive Discipline." Program Two: "Class Meetings, the Forum of Positive Discipline." Sandy, UT: *The Video Journal of Education*, volume VI, issue 7, 1997. (1-800-572-1153)

Walton, F. X. *Winning Teenagers Over.* Columbia, SC: Adlerian Child Care Books.

Index

A

ABC Groups
  job descriptions, 199–200
  typical problems, 200–201
Accountability, 166
Acknowledgments, 53
Actions instead of words, 174–175
Adaptability, 9
Adler, Alfred, 39
Adult Children of Dysfunctional
  Classrooms (ACDCs), xi–xii
Adultisms, 24
Agenda, 38
  creating agendas, 53–55
  defining problem in, 122–123
  in elementary school, 137–138
  follow-up on, 115–117
  at high school level, 143–144
  need for, 142–143
  revenge and, 156
  role playing and brainstorming, 88
  students named in, 115
  tattle-telling on, 141–142
  Wheel of Choice on, 54
Appreciations, 53
  after brainstorming, 96
  on death of student, 98–99
  in parent/teacher/student
    conferences, 179–180
  in Teachers Helping Teachers, 196
Appropriate choices, 160–161
Approval junkies, 104
Asking students, 168–169
Assumed inadequacy, 78
Assumptions
  caring, barrier to, 20–21
  testing assumptions, 21
Attitudes, 29–30
Authoritarian methods, 14

B

Backhanded compliments, 51, 141
Bayton, Carter, 19–20
Behavior Songs (Frieden &
  Hartwell-Walker), 84
Birth order, 189–190
Blame, concept of, 61
Brainstorming, 88, 91–95
  on classroom jobs, 161–162
  format for, 116
  long-range solutions, 94
  role playing and, 93
  silliness and, 92
  on solutions, 106–107
  Teachers Helping Teachers and,
    194–195
  on time outs, 177–178

C

Candle activity, 74–77
Capabilities. *See* Personal capabilities
Caring, 17–18
  attitudes and skills, 26–33
  barriers to, 20–26
  builders of, 20–26
  perception of, 19
  power of, 19–20
  rescuing/explaining barrier, 21–22
  respect and, 24–26
Celebrating accomplishments, 23–24
Challenging students, 186–187
Checking and caring, 21

Children: The Challenge
(Dreikurs), 127
Choices, 160–161
  limited choices, 160–161
  poor solutions, choice of, 143
Chore charts, 163
Circle, forming a, 47–50
Class meetings, 3–5. *See also* Agendas
  agenda items, 38
  building blocks for, 37–55, 41–42
  buying in to, 42–43
  caring in, 33–35
  circle, forming a, 47–50
  citizenship and, 13–14
  compliments, practicing, 49–53
  criteria for, 40–41
  daily class meetings, 44–46
  in difficult situations, 97–99
  enthusiasm for, 119–120
  exploring in, 22
  feedback from, 39–41
  follow-up in, 114
  format for, 47, 114
  future plans made in, 117–119
  guidelines for, 62–63
  immaturity and, 139–140
  on life issues, 25
  making time for, 10–11
  on outside problems, 96–97
  regularly scheduled meetings, 38
  review of building blocks, 113–114
  same problems, dealing with, 151
  separate realities and, 64–69
  skill-building for, 120
  solutions, focus on, 40
  talking sticks, use of, 41
  training in process, 41
  unwilling teachers/students, 142
  voting, 95
  weekly class meetings, 46–47
Classroom-Induced School Phobia,
  xi–xii
Classroom jobs
  list of, 32
  as management tool, 161–163
  routines for, 131
Clifton, Donald O., 180

Communication skills, 6, 57–69
  activities for, 59
  "I" statements, 60–61
  respect and, 61–62
  separate realities and, 64–69
  solutions, concept of, 61
  steps for, 57–58
  turn taking, 59–60
  win-win situations, 62
Compassion, 6
  severe discipline problems
    and, 153
Compliance, 102
Compliments
  backhanded, 51, 141
  embarrassment and, 140–141
  monotonous compliments,
    148–149
  practicing compliments, 49–53
  responding to, 51–52
  specificity in, 50–51
Computer games, 125
Conferences, parent/teacher/
  student, 178–181
Confidence, 6
Consequences, 18
  logical consequences, 106–107,
    203–210
Cooling-off period, 123
Criticisms, compliments as, 51

D
Daily class meetings, 44–46
Death, dealing with, 98–99
Decisions and control, 171–174
Defining problems, 122–123
Detentions, 18, 102
Dignity
  follow-through with, 165–168
  saying no with, 174
Directives, 22–23
Discipline problems, severe, 151–154
Discouragement, 71
Discussion, encouragement of, 43–44
Disrespect, 32
Dixon, Judy, 129
Do-nothing idea, 170–171

INDEX

Dreikurs, Rudolf, 1, 17, 37, 39, 57, 71, 72, 87, 92, 99, 101, 104, 106, 113, 121, 127, 135, 159, 165, 185
Duffy, Rosalyn, 3, 64, 118, 180

E
Elementary teachers, questions by, 136–138
Embarrassment, 18
Emotional Intelligence (Goleman), ix
Emotional issues, 123
Empowering Others: Ten Keys to Affirming and Validating People (Glenn), 20
Empowering perceptions, 7
Encouragement, 23
  activities for, 81–85, 130–131
  chart, 83
  in parent/teacher/student conferences, 179–180
  praise and, 127–131
  rewards and, 127–131
  teachers, meetings for, 187–188
Enjoyment of teaching, 28–29
Escobar, Linda, 3, 64, 118, 180
Essential skills, 7
Expectations, 23
Explaining barrier, 21–22
Exploring, 22
External reward system, 12

F
Facilitators in Teachers Helping Teachers, 199
Family Songs (Frieden & Hartwell-Walker), 74
The Family That Works Together (Lott & Intner), 3
Feedback, 39–41
  encouragement through, 128
Feelings
  hurt feelings, 126–127
  "I" statements and, 60–61
  role playing and, 91
  time outs and, 177
Field trip planning, 117–119
First-grade class meetings, 149–150

Fixing problems, 176
Fix time, 123
Flexibility, 9
Following-through
  dignity and respect in, 165–168
  steps for effective follow–through, 166
  traps, 167–168
Four Mistaken Goals of Behavior, 2, 72
  activity for, 78–81
  candle activity and, 74–77
  chart of, 73
  encouragement, activities for, 81–85
  teaching students about, 74–77
Four Rs of Solutions, 108–109
Frieden, Wayne, 75, 84
Friends, sitting by, 139
Future plans, 117–119

G
Gemeinschaftsgefühl, definition of, 39
Glenn, H. Stephen, 6, 20, 168, 176
Goleman, Daniel (*Emotional Intelligence*), ix
Grades, encouragement about, 130
Graffiti problems, 34
Grounding, 18, 104
Grunwald, Bronia, 99–100
Guessing games, 89

H
Happiness, 6
Hartwell-Walker, Marie, 75, 84
Hiding mistakes, 125
High schools
  class meetings in, 45–46
  questions of teachers in, 139–144
Home life, 13
Homework
  attitude about, 27–28
  as punishment, 18
  reasons for not doing, 77–78
Humiliating students, 136–137

Humor. *See* Sense of humor
Hurt feelings, 126–127
Hygiene problems, 98

I
Ignoring problems, 163
Improvement, encouragement on, 33
Incorporating other strategies, 157–158
Influence, perception of, 7, 8
Integrity, 9
Interpersonal skills, 9
Intner, Riki, 3
Intrapersonal skills, 7, 8–9
Inviting, 23
Involving students, 32–33
"I" statements, 60–61

J
Jenkins, James Mancel, 18
Judgment skills, 9
Junior high schools. *See* Middle schools

K
Kangaroo courts, 40
Kindergarten class meetings, 147–148
Kohn, Alphie, 12

L
Learning disabilities, 4
Learning from mistakes, 121, 123–126
Lecturing, 38
routines and, 133
Lesk, Earl, 34–35
Listening. *See also* Communication skills
buddies, 178
to students, 27–28
Logical consequences, 106–107, 203–210
advanced planning for, 207–208
of choices, 210
misuse of, avoiding, 203–208

piggybacking, avoidance of, 206–207
teaching students about, 208–210
Lott, Lynn, 3, 5, 55, 126, 186
Lunch detention, 18

M
Maintaining Sanity in the Classroom (Grunwald, Dreikurs & Pepper), 99
Management tools, 159–183
chart of, 183
Mann, Kent, 168
Meder, Frank, 33–34
Middle schools
class meetings in, 45
compliments, practicing, 52–53
questions of teachers in, 139–144
Mistaken Goals of Behavior. *See* Four Mistaken Goals of Behavior
Mistakes
hiding mistakes, 125
learning from, 121, 123–125
solutions as, 143
Three Rs of Recovery from, 126–127
Motivation, 6
punishment and, 103–104
Mutual respect, 2
foundation of, 10

N
Name-calling, 164
Natural consequences, 170–171
Nelsen, Jane, 3, 5, 6, 20, 55, 64, 118, 126, 168, 176, 180, 186
question-and-answer session with, 144–158
Nelson, Paula, 180
Nicknames for students, 29
Nicoll, William, xi
No, saying, 174
Note-passing, 139

O
Observers in Teachers Helping Teachers, 199

Ortolano, Kate, 3, 64, 118, 184
Outside classroom problems, 96–97
Outside interests of students,
    31–32
Owen-Sohocki, Debbie, 3, 64,
    118, 184

P

Parent/teacher/student
    conferences, 178–181
Pepper, Floy, 99
Perfectionism, 33, 89
Permissiveness, 64
Personal capabilities, 6
    perception of, 7–8
Planning classroom activities,
    117–119
Platt, Ann Roeder, 34
Positive Discipline (Nelsen), 3, 187
Positive Discipline for Teenagers (Nelsen
    & Lott), 3, 126, 187
*Positive Discipline in the Classroom:
    A Teacher's A–Z Guide* (Nelsen,
    Duffy, Escobar, Ortolano &
    Owen–Sohocki), 3, 64, 118,
    180, 187
*Positive Discipline in the Classroom
    Featuring Class Meetings*, 144
Positive Discipline in the Classroom
    (Nelsen & Lott)
    manual, 55, 187
    Video Journal, 4
Positive time outs. *See* Time outs
Posters, 52
    on punishment, 104
    on respect, 62
    on solutions, not blame, 61
    We Decided poster, 63
Power, 78
    perception of, 7, 8
Praise, 129
Preaching, 38
Privileges, removing, 105
Problem-solving skills, 6, 87–100
    intrapersonal skills and, 8–9
    steps for, 163–165
    student participation and, 11–12

Teachers Helping Teachers,
    188–196
Project ACCEPT, 147
Punished by Rewards (Kohn), 12
Punishments, 12. *See also* Rewards
    common forms of, 102
    elimination of, 103
    false premises of, 101–102
    long-range effects, 102
    motivation and, 103–104
    permissiveness as alternative, 64

Q

Questions
    frequently asked questions,
        144–158
    redirection questions, 169–170

R

*Raising Self-Reliant Children in a
    Self-Indulgent World* (Glenn &
    Nelsen), 6, 20, 26, 168
Rasmussen, Robert, 28–29
Reacting, 171–174
Reasons for behavior, 77–85
Rebellion, 102
Redirection questions, 169–170
Referrals, 18
Rescuing
    barrier, 21–22
    routines and, 133
Respect. *See also* Mutual respect
    brainstorming and, 92–93
    caring and, 24–26
    communication skills and, 61–62
    following-through with, 165–168
    for outside interests of students,
        31–32
    saying no with, 174
    self-respect, 5
    solutions and, 111–112
Responsibility, 5, 9
Revenge, 78, 82–83
    agenda as, 156
Rewards, 12–13. *See also* Punishments
    encouragement instead of,
        127–131

Rewards *(continued)*
  field trips and, 118–119
Risk-taking, 5
Ritter, Janice, 144–158
Rogers, Kay, 111–112, 144–158
Role playing, 88, 89–91
  brainstorming and, 93
  responses to, 91
  for routines, 132
  Teachers Helping Teachers and,
    192–194, 195
Routines, 131–132
  guidelines for, 132–133
Rules, posting of, 146–147

S
Safety issues, 48
Same boat, putting students in,
  175–176
Same problems, dealing with, 151
Saturday school, 18
School bus, misbehavior on, 96–97
Scolding, 105
Seating in classroom, 139
Self-confidence, 5
Self-control, 5
Self-discipline, 5
Self-esteem, 3, 5
  compliments and, 49
  mistakes and, 124
  punishment and, 104
Self-worth, 104
Sense of humor, 6
  caring and, 30–31
Separate realities, 64–69
  activities on, 65–69
  subconscious decisions based on,
    71–72
Significance, perception of, 7, 8
Significant Seven, 6–10
Sixth-grade class meetings,
  139–140
Small steps, 181–182
Smith, Bonnie G., 129
Soar with Your Strengths (Clifton &
  Nelson), 180
Social interest, 38–39

Solutions
  activities for focusing on, 103–106
  brainstorming and, 91–95,
    106–107
  communications skills and, 61
  in elementary classes, 138
  encouragement and, 128
  focus on, 40, 101–112
  follow-up on, 114
  Four Rs of Solutions, 108–109
  guiding to appropriate solutions,
    154–155
  nonpunitive solutions, 103–112
  poor solutions, choice of, 143
  Wheel of Choice, 110–111
Spanking, 105
Special education classes, 98, 141
Special event planning, 117–119
Survival behavior, 72
Suspensions, 18, 102
Systemic skills, 9

T
Talking over problems, 163–164
Talking sticks, 41
  for compliments, 52
Talk time, 123
Tardy students, 31–32
Tattle-telling
  agenda and, 141–142
  in class meeting, 150
Teachers Helping Teachers,
  185–201
  ABC Groups, 199–201
  appreciations, 196
  brainstorming in, 194–195
  choosing solutions, 195
  commitment by teacher, 196
  Encouragement Meetings,
    187–188
  identifying feelings, 191
  job descriptions, 199–200
  problem-solving with, 188–196
  role playing in, 192–194, 195
  short guide to problem-solving,
    197–198
Telling students, 168–169

Three Rs of Recovery from mistakes, 126–127
Time Out: Abuses and Effective Uses (Nelsen & Glenn), 168, 176
Time outs, 176–178
  guidelines for, 178
Tone of voice, 27
Training for class meetings, 41
Tunney, James Joseph, 18–19
Turn taking, 59–60

U
Understanding: Eliminating Stress and Finding Serenity in Life and Relationships (Nelsen), 64
Undue attention, 78
Uniqueness, appreciation of, 29

V
Vandalism, 33–34

Video games, 125
Video Journal, 4
Violence in school, 33–34
Voice, tone of, 27
Volunteers in Teachers Helping Teachers, 199
Voting, 95

W
We Decided poster, 63
Weekly class meetings, 46–47
Wheel of Choice
  on agenda, 54
  use of, 110–111
Win-win situations, 62
  agreement on solutions as, 164
Workshops, 5

Positive Discipline A-Z

1001 Solutions to Everyday Parenting Problems

Jane Nelsen

Lynn Lott

H. Stephen Glenn

U.S. $14.95

Can. $19.95

ISBN 1-55958-312-6

paperback / 368 pages

What should I do when she has a temper tantrum in the grocery store?

What should I do when he bites another child?

What should I do when she won't go to bed at night?

What should I do when he won't eat his dinner?

Wouldn't it be nice if there was a book that listed in alphabetical order every childraising problem parents could imagine? Here it is—from bestselling parenting experts. This book not only helps parents solve problem behaviors, it also helps children feel good about themselves, gain self-confidence and self-discipline, learn responsibility, and develop problem-solving skills.

Positive Discipline for Preschoolers

For Their Early Years—Raising Children Who Are Responsible, Respectful, and Resourceful

Jane Nelsen
Cheryl Erwin
Roslyn Duffy

U.S. $14.00
Can. $18.95
ISBN 1-55958-497-1
paperback / 336 pages

Positive Discipline for Preschoolers offers real solutions for every parent and teacher of young children. In this practical book you'll find loving, affirming tools of communication and discipline designed specifically to address interaction between adults and preschoolers, during the most important years of a child's development. Critical topics include:

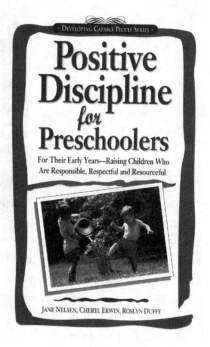

• Mastering preschooler challenges—sleeping, eating, and potty training

• Encouraging positive behavior at home, preschool, and daycare

• Developing logical consequences that are related, respectful, and reasonable.

Positive Discipline
for Teenagers

Resolving Conflict with Your Teenage Son or Daughter

Jane Nelsen, Ed.D.
Lynn Lott, M.A., M.F.C.C.

U.S. $14.95
Can. $19.95
ISBN 1-55958-441-6
paperback / 448 pages

For both teenagers and parents the teen years can be like living in a war zone. This book offers parents practical solutions for turning off the cycle of guilt and blame and working toward greater communication with their adolescents. With this book, you'll learn:

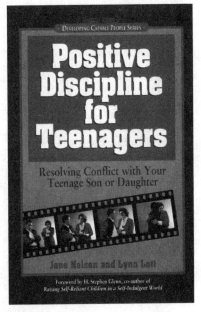

• How to win cooperation without having to threaten
• How to tell if your teen's rebellion is normal or excessive
• How to see the world through the eyes of your teenager
• How you and your teen can grow and change together
• How to nurture your teenager's need for independence

ORDER FORM

To: Empowering People, P.O. Box 1926, Orem, UT 84059
Phone: 1-800-456-7770 (credit card orders only) Fax: 801/762-0022

BOOKS	Price	Quantity	Amount
Positive Discipline in the Classroom by Nelsen, Lott & Glenn	$14.95		
Positive Discipline: A Teacher's A-Z Guide by Nelsen, Duffy, Escobar, Ortolano & Owen-Sohocki	$14.95		
Positive Discipline A-Z by Nelsen, Lott & Glenn	$14.95		
Raising Self-Reliant Children in a Self-Indulgent World by Glenn & Nelsen	$12.95		
Positive Discipline for Teenagers by Nelsen & Lott	$14.95		
Positive Discipline by Nelsen	$11.00		
Positive Discipline for Single Parents by Nelsen, Erwin & Delzer	$12.95		
Positive Discipline for Preschoolers by Nelsen, Erwin & Duffy	$14.00		
Time Out: Abuses & Effective Uses by Nelsen & Glenn	$6.95		
Understanding: Eliminating Stress... by Nelsen	$12.00		
Positive Discipline for Parenting in Recovery by Nelsen, Intner & Lott	$12.95		
The Family That Works Together... by Lott & Intner	$9.95		
To Know Me Is To Love Me by Lott, Kentz & West	$10.00		
Together and Liking It by Lott and West	$7.95		
TAPES & VIDEOS			
Positive Discipline cassette tape	$10.00		
Positive Discipline video	$49.95		
Building Healthy Self-Esteem through Positive Discipline by Nelsen	$10.00		
Positive Discipline in the Classroom cassette tapes	$49.95		
Positive Discipline in the Classroom video	$9.95		
MANUALS			
Teaching Parenting the Positive Discipline Way	$39.95		
Positive Discipline for Parenting in Recovery	$19.95		
Positive Discipline for Single Parents	$19.95		
Positive Discipline for Preschoolers	$19.95		
Positive Discipline in the Classroom	$39.95		
Student Assistance through Positive Discipline	$19.95		

SUBTOTAL _____

Sales tax: UT add 6.25% ; CA add 7.25% _____

Shipping & Handling: $2.50 plus 50¢ for each item _____

TOTAL _____

(Prices subject to change without notice.)

METHOD OF PAYMENT (check one):

_____ Check made payable to Empowering People Books, Tapes & Videos
_____ Mastercard, Visa, Discover Card, American Express

Card #_____ Expiration _____/_____
Ship to_____
Address_____
City/State/Zip_____
Daytime Phone_____